The Gardens of Los Poblanos

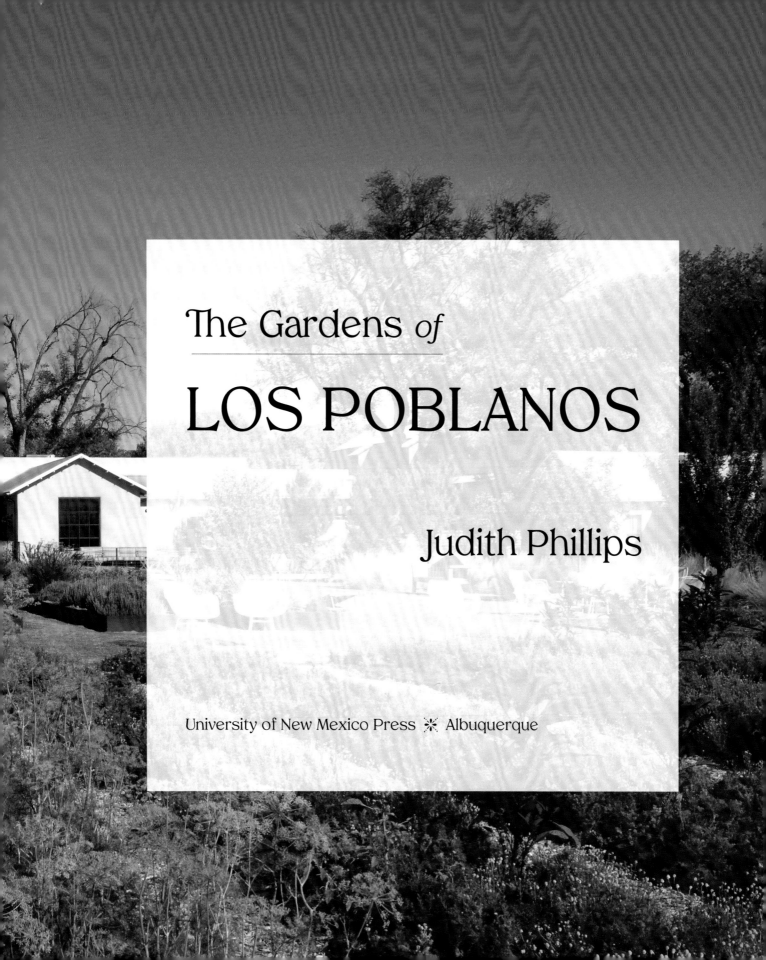

The Gardens *of*

LOS POBLANOS

Judith Phillips

University of New Mexico Press ✳ Albuquerque

NEW CENTURY GARDENS AND LANDSCAPES
OF THE AMERICAN SOUTHWEST

Baker H. Morrow, *Series Editor*

Whether practical gardening guides, best plant
guides, landscape architecture showcases, or blue-
prints for urban ecology, books in the New Century
Gardens and Landscapes of the American Southwest series address the challenges novice gardeners
and skilled practitioners alike face with prolonged
droughts, limited water supplies, high-altitude
climes, and growing urbanization. Books in this
series not only provide practical landscaping advice
for backyard gardeners, they dive deep into ecology,
built environments, agricultural history, and the
emerging discipline of urban ecology. The New
Century Gardens and Landscapes of the American
Southwest series tackles the environmental questions
that many communities in the American West con-
front as we all work to create healthy, dynamic, and
inviting outdoor spaces.

Also available in the New Century Gardens and
Landscapes of the American Southwest Series:

*Water for the People: The Global Heritage of New
Mexico's Acequias* edited by Enrique A. Lamadrid
and José A. Rivera

Names: Phillips, Judith, 1949– author.
Title: The gardens of Los Poblanos / Judith Phillips.
Other titles: New century gardens and landscapes of
    the American Southwest.
Description: Albuquerque: University of New Mexico Press,
    [2023] | Series: New century gardens and landscapes of the
    American Southwest.
Identifiers: LCCN 2023005002 (print) |
    LCCN 2023005003 (ebook) | ISBN 9780826365224 (cloth) |
    ISBN 9780826365231 (epub)
Subjects: LCSH: Gardening—Rio Grande Valley (Colo.—
    Mexico and Tex.)—History. | Gardens—Rio Grande Valley
    (Colo.—Mexico and Tex.)—History. | Los Poblanos Histor-
    ic District (Los Ranchos de Albuquerque, N.M.)
Classification: LCC SB451.34.N6 P45 2023 (print) |
    LCC SB451.34.N6 (ebook) | DDC 635.09764/4—dc23/
    eng/20230215
LC record available at https://lccn.loc.gov/2023005002
LC ebook record available at https://lccn.loc.gov/2023005003

Founded in 1889, the University of New Mexico sits on the
traditional homelands of the Pueblo of Sandia. The original
peoples of New Mexico—Pueblo, Navajo, and Apache—since
time immemorial have deep connections to the land and have
made significant contributions to the broader community state-
wide. We honor the land itself and those who remain stewards of
this land throughout the generations and also acknowledge our
committed relationship to Indigenous peoples. We gratefully
recognize our history.

Cover photograph by Maura Casados
Designed by Felicia Cedillos
Composed in EB Garamond

This story is dedicated to the stewards
of the land along the Rio Grande since
8000 BCE

Contents

Foreword

MATT REMBE

Cultural landscapes are ultimately about people, not plants. Landscapes reflect the culture of people who lived there—how they lived, how they interacted with the land, what they grew, and their values. Los Poblanos has become a singular cultural landscape, shaped not only by New Mexico's rich culture and the Rio Grande Valley but also by architects, gardeners, farmers, chefs, innkeepers, beekeepers, and even visitors, who come from all over the world to experience what makes it unique. But it wasn't always that way. Local New Mexico horticulture legend Judith Phillips has played a very important role in how the landscape at Los Poblanos has been preserved and how it has evolved over the last fifteen years. While my family set out on a very deliberate mission to preserve the gardens at Los Poblanos and endeavors to perpetuate its agricultural history, we never imagined it would become recognized as an important cultural landscape.

I grew up at Los Poblanos, along with my older sister, Emily, and two older brothers, Armin and Jay. It was very much a Huck Finn type of childhood—truly magical. It was no longer a real ranch at that point, but *ranch* had been part of its name for more than fifty years, so that's what we always called it. It was more like a little farm estate—twenty-five acres of lush gardens, green lawns, giant cottonwood trees, stone acequias, rundown barns, and open fields of alfalfa, all nestled in the heart of the Rio Grande Valley. The entrance then was the same as it is today—a majestic tree-lined allée that split the property into two halves: a more formal half designed for cultural events and a residential half combined with a real working farm. That's the half my parents bought from the Simms family in 1977, and it has been their home ever since. There were orchards, rose gardens, vegetable gardens, a greenhouse, a hay barn, a wine cellar, dilapidated dairy buildings, a duck pond, and corrals and pens for the animals. The territorial revival buildings looked out toward the Sandia Mountains, with their backs against the Griegos Lateral, the irrigation ditch that fed from the Rio Grande, only several hundred yards behind it and the lifeblood of this valley for centuries. The entire North Valley was our playground, and Los Poblanos was the center of it all.

Although we grew up with very little to worry about, our parents did instill in us the ethic of work early on. We all had daily chores—tending to chickens, pigs, goats, and sheep. On weekends we had to clean the pens before we could play with our friends, many of whom lived within a mile and were a constant presence at the ranch. We rode our bikes everywhere, up and down the acequias and along the river, being careful not to get run over by dirt bikers, whose motors' beelike swarming sounds were as common as the cicadas and toads. We filled up our bike tires at an old Chevron station only a few hundred yards down Rio Grande Boulevard. Just to the north was "Dead Man's Curve," a sharp turn in the road that most people knew as Buffalo Curve, named for a herd of buffalo that grazed alongside the two-lane road. The turn was sharp enough to be precarious on its own, but the added distraction of seeing a herd of buffalo while you made the hairpin turn only contributed to the problem. My dad was a doctor and more than once had to extract someone who had wrecked their motorcycle on the whitewashed farm fence that separated the curve from our fields.

We had rope swings over the acequias and played football on the little sand bed islands in the Rio Grande. On summer nights we rounded up more than a dozen kids to play cagey-cagey, our version of capture the flag; we jailed captured players in an old hog cage among the farm buildings. And like many rural youngsters, we were allowed to drive on the farm at a fairly young age. Enough hours logged on the John Deere rider mower somehow afforded me the right to drive a little pickup truck anywhere on the farm. After school, my fellow sixth-graders clung on for dear life in the back of the truck as I took corners at full throttle and cranked the emergency brake on the gravel to see if I could shake anyone loose. Luckily, nobody died during all these adventures, although we did experience the occasional broken leg (me) or someone getting kicked in the face by a horse (me again).

Despite both of my parents having demanding jobs, they somehow found plenty of time to devote to the farm and gardens. On any given weeknight, they spent time watering, pruning, weeding, and killing squash bugs or aphids, usually with a cold Coors beer can in one hand. Those evenings were often weeknights and the risk of being put to work was low, so it a nice time to just be together. We weren't really a family that gathered around the dinner table for deep conversation, so it was rare when we all slowed down like that in one place. It wasn't until many years later that I realized how important that time was for my parents' relationship. Apart from doing something they both equally loved, it was cathartic for my father, who as an oncologist faced pain and suffering every day. It also made space for my mother to share her day with him, as he left early in the morning, when it was still dark. They never took living at Los Poblanos for granted. They recognized how special it was, shared it with the community at every opportunity, and expressed a deep gratitude for living there by devoting the rest of their lives to stewardship of Los Poblanos. My parents remained happily married for fifty-five years, until my father's passing in 2021.

My parents were heavily inspired and driven by the accomplishments of Ruth Simms, who along with her husband, Albert, conceived most of Los Poblanos Ranch. She accomplished so much in so little time, and it's daunting to think how many details she got right. In addition to selecting John Gaw Meem to oversee the architecture, she also hired pioneer landscape architect Rose Greely to design the gardens. It has truly taken our family a lifetime to understand what Ruth and Albert, together with John Gaw Meem, designed and built between in 1932 and 1937.

It is very surprising that Ruth Simms is still somewhat unknown in our state, but she has always been a hero of the tallest order in our family. Many New Mexico heroes are artists and writers, such as Paul Horgan, Will Shuster, Peter Hurd, and Mable Dodge Lujan. Others are lesser known, but they helped shape my parents' understanding of Los Poblanos Ranch. Architect John Gaw Meem unquestionably made the biggest impact, especially as he was a pioneer in historic preservation in a state with the oldest architecture in the country. There were also scholars like E. Boyd, who came to document New Mexico art as part of the New Deal, and Dorothy Doolittle, who wrote one of the first books on Southwest gardening. More recently, the list includes architectural historian Chris Wilson, author of the definitive book on John Gaw Meem, and Stanley Crawford, a novelist and garlic farmer who wrote on the primeval acequia systems that are disappearing during our lifetime. And very deserving to be on the list is the Southwest's foremost expert on plants—Judith Phillips. Judith has devoted her entire life to understanding our soil, our climate, our plants, and our entire ecosystem, much of which she has shared in her five books. When our family set out to create a long-range preservation plan for Los Poblanos Ranch, Judith was the obvious choice to help us with plant selections aligned with the history of Los Poblanos and our future goals for a more regenerative approach to horticulture. The work was much more challenging and complex than any of us thought, and twenty years later, Judith is the only person with the knowledge, expertise, and stamina to write this thorough history of Los Poblanos.

MATT REMBE,
executive director of Los Poblanos

Acknowledgments

Book projects are always collaborations, and because writing history is a new experience for me, I am especially grateful for the help of all the people who aided and abetted in bringing *The Gardens of Los Poblanos* to life.

Deepest thanks to Penny and Armin Rembe for sowing the seeds of preservation, and thanks to the whole Rembe family for generously allowing me a glimpse into their history in the making and for describing how the gardens have colored their lives. Matt Rembe offered insight into his vision that has allowed the ongoing preservation of Los Poblanos while making it the vibrant experience it is, and kudos to the teams of worker bees who guide that experience.

Thanks to Albert, Mary, and Frank Simms, who graciously answered my requests for memories of their time at Los Poblanos.

The Los Poblanos management team includes Wes Brittenham, director of horticulture; Maxfield Bervig, farm manager; Jonathan Perno, former executive chef; Christopher Bethoney, head chef; Jhette Gonzales-Duran, kitchen manager and food facility manager; and Jamie Lord, lead distiller. These talented and hardworking folks offered insights into their roles in furthering the mission at Los Poblanos. Lauren Kemner, former marketing manager; Amy Carrara, design and brand manager; and Kate Garner, culture and community event director, directed me to archival information included in these pages. Thanks to Katherine Trujillo, executive assistant, for fielding "just one more question" multiple times. I thank them all for adding a layered perspective to the daily workings of this dynamic place.

Archivists are the gatekeepers of history. Heather Riser from University of Virginia Special Collections, Jillian Hartke from the Albuquerque Museum of Art and History, Selena Capraro from the Amon Carter Museum of American Art, Leslie Kim, curator of history at the Albuquerque Museum of Art and History, and Audra Bellmore from the Center for Southwest Research at the University of New Mexico all opened their treasure troves and directed me to information and photographs that help illuminate the past and deepen the story.

Thanks to Pam McBride, paleoethnobotanist, and Marcia Newren, recovering archaeologist, for reading the backstory of the land that is Los Poblanos and clarifying how science reconstructs the past.

Thanks to Doug Strech and Yasmine Najmi with the Middle Rio Grande Conservancy District, who sought out the maps that illustrate the changes in land use at Los Poblanos and described the water conservation strategies MRGCD is implementing to assure farmers' access to the water needed to grow our food.

Many thanks to Hannah Aulick, landscape designer and graphic artist, who worked with me on the as-built site maps and bird's-eye views of the gardens of Los Poblanos in all their complexity, growing in beauty and adapting to a changing world.

Thanks to Stefanos Polyzoides, partner at Moule & Polyzoides, Architects and Urbanists, and cofounder of the Congress for the New Urbanism, and Shawn Evans, principal at Atkins Olshin and Schade Architects, for the use of their project graphics.

Thanks to Wes Brittenham, Douglas Merriam, Lauren Kemner, Hunter Ten Broeck, Baker Morrow, Carlos Alejandro, and Sergio Salvador for photographs that illustrate the story of the gardens.

Thanks to Baker Morrow for initiating this project. His esteem for the history of New Mexico and for the history and practice of landscape architecture has enriched many lives.

Thanks to Chris Wilson for deepening my understanding of the architectural and cultural layers at Los Poblanos.

Thanks to family and friends who have kindly listened to more about Los Poblanos in the past few years than anyone needs to.

Finally, many thanks to all the guests at Los Poblanos Inn and at Campo, and thanks to the shoppers who keep clearing the Farm Shop shelves of lavender salve and other products that have evolved from the idea that climate-adapted plants add value to lives along the Rio Grande and far beyond. I offer gratitude for your support of Los Poblanos. You make possible preservation of the historic hacienda and La Quinta and the future of farms and gardens growing along the Rio.

The Story of Los Poblanos

Wisdom sits in places.
—Dudley Patterson, Cibecue Apache elder

Los Poblanos Inn and Organic Farm—the gardens of Los Poblanos—occupies twenty-five acres of land near the Rio Grande northwest of Albuquerque in the village of Los Ranchos de Albuquerque. This is the ancestral land of the Tiguex peoples, whose descendants today are the Tue-I Isleta and Na-Fiat Sandia Puebloans. The ebb and flow of life here is a long and complex story of adaptation and innovation by both people and plants. The name Los Poblanos comes from early colonial settlers who came to New Mexico from Puebla, Mexico. These farmers were called *poblanos*. This land has been gardened in one way or another for ten thousand years, and

(*opposite page*) Bosque with moon. The ebb and flow of life along the Rio Grande is a long and complex story of adaptation and innovation by both people and plants. Since 1932 it has been the story of the gardens of Los Poblanos. Photograph by the author.

Los Poblanos is important to landscape architecture as one of the last remaining and accessible examples of Country Place landscapes in New Mexico, with architecture noteworthy in the history of New Mexico and gardens worthy of the architecture. The Country Place era in American landscape architecture began in the 1870s and was brought to a near standstill by the Great Depression. It was a time when the newly mega-wealthy financed the design and building of mansions on large rural landholdings, often as summer homes. These nouveau palaces were surrounded by equally resplendent gardens designed by the cream of American landscape architects, including Frederick Law Olmsted, the first American described as such, Beatrix Farrand, Jens Jensen, and, most pertinent to the story of the gardens of Los Poblanos, Rose Greely.

The work of John Gaw Meem and Rose Greely at Los Poblanos elevates the story of the gardens of

Los Poblanos to one of particular significance in the Country Place era. John Gaw Meem was one of the preeminent architects of the twentieth century in the Southwest. First trained in civil engineering in Virginia after a youth spent in Brazil, Meem came to New Mexico to recover from tuberculosis and quickly developed a deep appreciation of the simple beauty and climate-consciousness of the traditional adobe architecture he encountered there. His career combined adapting historic adobe architecture to modern uses while preserving its integrity with designing contemporary architecture that evoked regional traditions without trying to replicate them. Meticulous attention to detail and use of local materials as well as a new interpretation of ancient methods created his uniquely regional contemporary architecture, which came to be called Santa Fe style.

Rose Greely was one of the first women architects and landscape architects in the United States. She began her independent design career in 1925 at the height of the Country Place era, and she also wrote extensively for *House Beautiful* magazine, sharing her experience with an interested readership. Her broad background gave her a great facility for linking indoor and outdoor spaces. Although Los Poblanos is her only known project in the Southwest, her penchant for functionality and her ability to observe and assess similarities and differences in growing conditions served her remarkably well when working in an ecosystem so different than that of the East Coast. Together with property owner Ruth Simms, Meem and Greely created a lasting legacy at Los Poblanos, elevating a beautiful working ranch to a noteworthy country place. The Simms–Greely collaboration at Los Poblanos is still vital today.

Because of the people involved, Los Poblanos has always been an international crossroads in the once remote and ever idiosyncratic desert Southwest. There is abundant archaeological evidence of brisk and far-reaching communications and trade between the Ancestral Puebloans of the Rio Grande Valley, the people of present-day Mexico, and likely peoples farther south in the Americas. Since Theodore Roosevelt visited in the Simms era, Los Poblanos has hosted political leaders from presidents to ambassadors, mayors, and councilors, artists from muralists to musicians, poets and painters, academics, actors and farmers, doctors and lawyers, tech wizards, scientists, and neighbors and their families. The diverse guest list reflects the influence this garden and its stewards have had over time. The present gardens of Los Poblanos are tended by farmers who see the land as their living and life-giving mother in the spirit of the earliest farmers. The farmers partner with chefs offering inspired preparation and alfresco servings of locally grown foods. Both farmers' and chefs' missions are to feed people well. The gardens have a history of providing a taste of the cultures and traditions of New Mexico. Whether restful and contemplative or sensory and exploratory, guests today are surrounded by plants that feed the body and soul.

Although much has been written about the architecture of Los Poblanos, very little has been documented about the gardens. Even early photographs focus on the buildings, with only passing glimpses of the surrounding landscape. Having been designed and built well, and continuously well cared for, the historic buildings tell many wonderful stories. While it is apropos that the architecture of John Gaw Meem is celebrated, the landscape nestled beneath cottonwoods, crosscut by acequias and lush with blooming and edible plantings, is a large part of the appeal of this place. I am gratified to have been involved in the landscape planning for the transition of the historic gardens to present-day Los Poblanos, enthusiastic because I knew the gardens were essential in its past and would be as important as the architecture in its future. I am honored to tell this story of the gardens. This is the saga of the many influences that the owners, designers, and gardeners have had on the evolution of the gardens. It is also the story of the impact the gardens have had on the preservation of agrarian roots in the neighboring properties in the village of Los Ranchos and well beyond, and in the paradigm shift from exploitation back to resiliency.

Querencia is a metaphysical concept expressed in a single Spanish word. The most common local meaning is having a strong relationship to a place and a personal identification with it, finding a safe haven and a feeling of belonging to that place. The name Los Poblanos could be used as a synonym. Perhaps it is the glimpse back in time that captures the imagination or the careful plans for future resilience that restore our hope. Certainly, it is the seasonal menus at Campo, the restaurant; the latent scent of lavender mingling with old roses in summer or piñon woodsmoke; and the chortling sounds of sandhill cranes in winter that call us home. Querencia is the reason Los Poblanos has persisted so wonderfully intact through time, created and stewarded by the generous people who have lovingly cared for this place and who graciously share it with others.

In these days of more extreme extremes in climate, the gardens are a nearly century-long timeline of the changes in landscape style and content driven by cultural expectations and climatic realities. Although plants are always my personal focus, gardens are more than plants, and plants are much more than mere fillers of garden space. The way the land is apportioned and the way it is used have driven and continue to spur the planting choices. Cultural values and the spirit of the time are strong

influences. The most recent planning and planting for the phases of the evolution at Los Poblanos included keeping the landscape a coherent whole, which meant adopting plants growing in the existing gardens that have thrived there over time, blending them with more heat- and drought-adapted species that will be resilient, demanding fewer resources into the future, and balancing water use with food value—nourishing with beauty and taste. In other words, the program was to be mindful of past successes and to guide the gardens into a vital tomorrow, "rooted in history; planting seeds for the future."

Some of the layouts and many of the plants chosen to fulfill those goals have changed considerably over the last one hundred years. Yet it is remarkable how much has been maintained given the changes in how the garden has been used and the people using it over time. Early in human history here, the landscape was essentially what nature provided. As cultivating useful native plants evolved into small-scale agriculture, coaxing crops and gleaning medicines out of this arid land left little time for ornamentals. Unbiased by human cultural values, all plants are valuable in some way. Birds and bees appraise the landscape much differently than do humans. In addition to the saturated flower color that lures pollinators, many desert plants combine architectural forms with aromatic foliage that can be diaphanous, sometimes ephemeral—qualities that draw people into the garden. The unadorned native landscape has a raw elegance that perhaps satisfied any need for enhancement that weary farmers could muster after a long day's labor. The sun rising over a wash of sunflowers in the 1400s, a flooded cornfield in the 1800s, or flowers abuzz with bees in the rows of lavender today, or the watermelon pink light on the Sandia Mountains at sunset then and now—the beautiful thread of gardening has never been broken, although what is grown has evolved. I use the term *gardening* as an umbrella for tending plants, whether farming for food or for the beauty of the plants in a designed setting, whether on a small plot or on many acres. Landscape, in the telling of this story, is the larger ecosystem that provides context for the tended gardens.

From colonial times, the influence on North America's gardens was from the Old World. The estates of the founders were stripped of their native plants and replanted with exotics from temperate zones across the planet, mostly funneled through Spain or England. Pampered exotics and acres devoted to lawns kept manicured by grazing sheep were signs of status in the early settlements of the eastern United States and later the Midwest. The Southwest has always been a cultural anomaly. The climate has made planting exotics a costly gamble. Plants need to be adapted to diurnal fluctuations in temperature of fifty degrees Fahrenheit, single-digit humidity, dust-laden desiccating wind, and periods of dry soil alternated with downpours that saturate the ground. The survivors are tough, many of them are natives, and all are more likely to thrive once they are well rooted. Gambling gardeners hedge their bets. Taking advantage of summer monsoonal moisture when it comes, planting species that are out of their comfort zones in the cooler or warmer wind-protected locations they need to endure, watering adequately, and improving soil health rather than forcing growth with harsh chemicals are all strategies that can broaden the plant palette beyond locally native species when necessary or culturally expected.

Early in the urbanization of Albuquerque, the horticultural hype was that if you changed the conditions enough—acidify the soil or at the very least amend it copiously with organic matter, which is slow to develop in desert soils and is quickly

exhausted; buffer the wind with walls and fences; and water, water, water—you could grow just about anything here. Although the city has a vast and deep aquifer, once sold by developers as "the size of Lake Superior," the aquifer is not an inland sea of water; it is a mix of water, soils, and gravels, some of which are much less productive for the mining of water. Look at the undeveloped desert surrounding Albuquerque and understand that if Lake Superior seems too good to be true, it is because it is a mirage. The comparison might be more akin to a subterranean Aral Sea. And climate change is sunburning the emperor who has no clothes.

I came to the Southwest with gardening experience in the Midwest, book knowledge of the plants native here, and descriptions of the relationships Native peoples had with them. For as long as I can remember, I have always been aware of the plants around me—the copper beeches, carpets of moss, tiny flavor-packed wild strawberries, and raspberries that fed my childhood adventures in western New York. My grandfather always grew a big vegetable garden, and we harvested baskets of succulent peaches from my aunt's tree, but my first experiences of the bounty of the land were wild foraged, abundant, and soul-satisfying. When I found myself living amid the factory fields of corn and soybeans in Indiana, I sought out remnants of native vegetation, finding wild blackberries, shagbark hickories, and spring beauties in untillable drainage ways in the fields and along creeks. The southwestern landscape seemed so harsh by comparison, but I soon grew to respect and honor the plants growing here. Taken with the brilliant colors and soft textures of some plants and the prickly nature of others, I began to marvel at sunlight glinting off the gold or silver spines of cacti, the indelible imprint of agave leaves on each other as they unfolded, the pink haze of Apache plume and bush muhly seed heads. I was finally home and will gladly spend the rest of my life studying arid land plants with the endless inspiration they offer. The overarching lesson has been the value of diversity and reciprocity.

Early Native peoples understood that soil is alive, that the life of the soil is essential to plant health, and that people are nourished by the earth spiritually as well as physically. Present-day gardeners are only now relearning the importance of soil ecology. Native soils are symbiotic living systems; their microbial life supports and is supported by native plants. When growing exotic food crops, building, and maintaining soil health is essential not only for the vitality of the plants but also for the nutritional value that those plants are intended to provide. Beneficial microbes support plants by extending their root systems to tap a much greater soil area. In turn, greater access to moisture and elements in the soil gives microbes sugars they are not able to produce for themselves, since they lack chlorophyll. Healthy soils sequester more carbon and make the plants growing in them more productive and resilient. Improving soil health also extends to rangeland, where the sea of grasses supports much more life than livestock, which are the most obvious recipients of the bounty. The Simms family at Los Poblanos Ranch recognized that managing livestock to renew cover, rather than to deplete it and move on, is not only reasonable but also profitable.

The Rio Grande Valley has always been a place of agricultural experimentation, from the days of the Tiguex cultivating native food plants to the days of the Spanish colonists introducing plants culturally important to themselves. Since 1932, Los Poblanos has continued that tradition. The Simms had the money to invest in strategies for breeding cattle and sheep, selecting varieties of alfalfa, barley,

wheat, chrysanthemums, and roses that were better adapted and more productive to improve local farm and garden yields. While the value of water was not addressed directly in the Simms era, 1932 to 1964, the fourteen years from 1942 to 1956 were a period of extreme drought in a place where evaporation rates are always several times greater than average rainfall. The 1930s and 1940s were a time when turning on the tap and having water pour out freely was a relatively novel convenience. Acequias were still the primary irrigation sources, and beyond the acequias, dryland farming was the precarious norm. Water has been and continues to be viewed as a precious gift to use wisely.

We are now experiencing a period of greater than typical water deficits, and the present-day stewards of Los Poblanos Inn and Organic Farm are keen to implement water conservation strategies. Los Poblanos continues to be a place where innovation and adaptation come with the territory. Food, art, and history are celebrated. Guests are sheltered and entertained with care. While working to select plants for the gardens of Los Poblanos, I've been reacquainted with plants from my childhood and have worked to keep them viable while returning natives to the gardens. In the words of Steve Jobs, "You can't connect the dots looking forward; you can only connect them looking backward. So you have to trust that the dots will somehow connect in your future. You have to trust something—your gut, destiny, karma, whatever. This approach has never let me down and has made all the difference in my life." This is the ongoing evolution of the gardens of Los Poblanos. The story is divided into parts, beginning with the history of the people and plants in the Rio Grande Valley around 8000 BCE and spinning on to the Country Place era in American landscape architecture (1870s–1940s), the Simms country place at Los Poblanos (1932–1964),

Bocce court guineas and peacock. Preening peacocks and raucous guinea fowl are part of everyday life in the gardens of Los Poblanos. Photograph by Wes Brittenham.

the private family gardens (1965–2004), the new preservation model (2005–2014), the focus on the future (2015–2020), and 2021 onward.

Please use the table of contents as a timeline of the story of Los Poblanos as it adapts, trusting its future while honoring its roots. The sources and "invitation to dig deeper" at the end of each chapter offer opportunities to follow parts of the story further than a single book allows. I hope you will meander down the garden paths of these sources and become immersed in their unfolding stories.

Sources, and an Invitation to Dig Deeper

Keith H. Basso. *Wisdom Sits in Places: Landscape and Language Among the Western Apache.* Albuquerque: University of New Mexico Press, 1996.

CHAPTER 1

The History of Gardening in the Rio Grande Valley

Lives are frequently worlds apart, and it takes wisdom and patience to bridge such gaps . . . the power and force of culture cannot be, nor should be, repressed. It is the drive to keep ourselves comfortable by making others transform themselves into clones of ourselves that is so destructive. This is doubly so when we are not even aware of it.

—Edward T. Hall, cultural anthropologist

In a harsh and unforgiving climate, proximity to the turbid waters of the Rio Grande has long made the site of present-day Los Poblanos an inviting place to live and grow. To best understand how the gardens of Los Poblanos came to be what they are now, it is useful to follow the flow of the river across time. Los Poblanos today occupies the original homeland of Tiguex peoples (ancestral Tiwa people), and we are gratefully following in the footsteps and cultivating the seedbeds of these early stewards of the land. This small acknowledgment of the first people is the beginning of an epic of resilience in the face of upheaval, loss, perseverance, and adaptation that spans ten thousand years, continuing into these uncertain times.

Picture a broad, flat plain dotted with groves of cottonwood trees, bordered on the west in many places by the steep rise of a dry mesa with volcanic cones looming on the horizon. To the east is a less abrupt rise of alluvial fans and fluvial terraces inclining upward into the foothills of the Sandia Mountains. The beginning of the human story, perhaps at Los Poblanos, more generally in the middle Rio Grande Basin, is the gradual transition of the ancestors of the Tiguex and the people of the nineteen remaining present-day Pueblos from a hunter-gatherer culture to the cultivation of plants for food, medicine, and ritual.

Radiocarbon-dated remains from campfires in the Rio Grande watershed circa 8000 BCE indicate that early Indigenous people led a peripatetic life, hunting large game and gathering wild plants. Over the next millennium, there were traceable shifts in ecosystem dynamics. Stressors such as a decline in megafauna, an increasing human population, and a warming climate may have led to change in Native lifeways. According to paleoecologist Paul S. Martin, whatever the impetus, nomadic hunter-gatherers began "their 7,000-year experiment with native plants, leading to increasingly skillful techniques of harvesting and gathering, to the domestication of certain weedy camp-followers, and within the last 1,000 years, to the widespread adoption of flood plain agriculture."

Although the meandering nature of the Rio Grande, its flooding and receding, makes archaeological evidence of human activity in its floodplain spotty at best, the scarcity of reliable surface water in the desert and the sediment-enriched soil that the Rio Grande deposited make it likely that the valley has been gardened intermittently since the transition of prehistoric communities from hunting and gathering to the cultivation of food crops. We are now experiencing a warming climate, which has been recorded in tree rings and wildfire burn scars and is immediately observable over decades in shifting populations of plants and animals. The change in climate from 8000 BCE to 1000 BCE, though much more gradual than what we are currently experiencing, can be mapped through fossil pollen analysis and a growing kit of scientific tools aimed at understanding the impact of climate on human history.

Tending plants for food and medicine was an innovation that yielded a more consistent food supply with fewer calories expended, greater stability, and time to develop skills beyond those needed for day-to-day survival. In the context of the arid Southwest, even with access to the water of the Rio Grande, stability was a very tenuous condition. Much local prehistory along the middle Rio Grande Valley involves variations on the themes of adaptation and resilience. Early people may have expanded their store of knowledge by watching how brother and sister animals fared after eating or avoiding unfamiliar plants, by sampling, and by learning how cooking improved digestibility and how colors could be extracted and fixed as dyes. We have libraries, Google, and Wikipedia. They had

curious minds, careful observation, and the threat of starvation to fuel innovation. Lessons passed from generation to generation in the oral tradition and distilled the wisdom of place. Across all New Mexico and the greater desert Southwest, the story is of early cultures developing in places where life was never easy and the climate was always extreme. Populations waxed and waned with better and worse times. Access to water was the ultimate constraint, but the people persisted and populations grew, artifacts became more refined, and lifeways became more complex.

Severe drought is currently stressing many mainstream agricultural systems, supported with fossil water from deep wells pumped at rates far exceeding recharge and with chemical fertilizers that destroy soil microflora. The current intense and prolonged drought is often compared to the mega-drought of the late 1200s, when more than a quarter century of minimal precipitation in the Southwest caused human migration to places that offered more consistent water. At that time, the Rio Grande meandered across a floodplain three miles wide, a mosaic of marshes, cottonwood and willow groves, and free-flowing water. In the Rio Abajo, the lower Rio Grande Valley south of Santa Fe, below La Bajada, the fertility of the land was renewed by sediment carried by seasonal flooding from spring snowmelt and from summer monsoons. Valley cottonwood (*Populus deltoides* spp. *wislizeni*) is one of the keystone species in the watershed wherever enough water is available to support its majestic canopy. Besides the cool shade and layers of wildlife habitat that cottonwoods provide, their buds and bark contain salicin, which breaks down into salicylic acid, an herbal medicine with a long history of use and the active ingredient in aspirin.

Evidence from basketry, potsherds, shell frag-

Valley cottonwood (*Populus deltoides* spp. *wislizeni*) is a keystone species in the watershed wherever enough water is available to support their majestic canopies. Besides the cool shade canopy and layers of wildlife habitat that cottonwoods provide, their buds and bark contain salicin, which breaks down into salicylic acid, an herbal medicine with a long history of use and the active ingredient in aspirin. Photograph by the author.

ments, and macaw feathers indicates extensive trade among Native peoples of the Southwest and Mexico, and by 1000 BCE Ancestral Puebloans were cultivating squash, maize, and beans introduced from Mexico in addition to native amaranth greens (*Amaranthus* spp.), Rocky Mountain bee plant (*Cleome serrulata*), and wild tobacco (*Nicotiana obtusifolia*). Bee plant is extremely nutritious but required long cooking time and drying into dense cakes that could be stored for years as starva-

tion rations. Bee plant processing and storing is an example of early people's keen awareness of their precarious hold on survival in an erratic and harsh environment. Maize was the staple that fed the good times; the bee plant kept people alive during the lean times.

Native tobacco is a different story. At some point, the local native *Nicotiana obtusifolia* was replaced by a much more potent early domesticate tobacco, *Nicotiana rustica*. A cultivated species

Bee plant. *Cleome serrulata* is cultivated as pollinator forage and because it is beautiful. It is extremely nutritious but requires a long cooking time. Early peoples dried it into dense cakes, which could be stored for years, an example of their keen awareness of their precarious hold on survival in an erratic and harsh environment. Maize was the staple that fed the good times; bee plant kept people alive during the lean times. Photograph by the author.

Santo Domingo tobacco. *Nicotiana rustica*, developed by Indigenous peoples of the Amazon rain forests six thousand to eight thousand years ago, spread throughout early farming communities and came to be known as Aztec tobacco in early Mexico. Eventually passed along to the tribes of the Rio Grande Valley, *Nicotiana* was an important ceremonial plant, used to petition the beings who bring rain, every desert farmer's focus. With several other medicinal uses, this potent herb was assimilated into the local foodshed. Photograph by the author.

developed by Indigenous peoples of the Peruvian and Bolivian rain forests six thousand to eight thousand years ago, it spread throughout the early farming communities and eventually to the tribes of the Rio Grande Valley, where *Nicotiana* was also an important ceremonial plant. *Nicotiana rustica*

seeds are now offered by seed companies as Santo Domingo tobacco and assimilated into the local foodshed.

Early crops were not grown as monocultures. Desirable native species were grown among the introduced edibles. Ricegrass (*Achnatherum* syn.

Yerba mansa. *Anemopsis californica* is native along the Rio Grande, where it carpets the soil in the shade of cottonwoods and has been valued as a potent medicinal plant by curanderas, or traditional healers. In the gardens of Los Poblanos, it is a beautiful aromatic groundcover. The deep roots penetrate heavy clay soil, making it more permeable. Photograph by the author.

Oryzopsis hymenoides), cota or Indian tea (*Thelesperma megapotamicum*), globemallows (*Sphaeralcea* spp.), yerba mansa (*Anemopsis californica*), fringed sage (*Artemisia frigida*), milkweeds (*Asclepias* spp.), Indian hemp (*Apocynum cannabinum*), devil's claw (*Proboscidea parviflora*), canaigre (*Rumex hymenosepalus*), groundcherry (*Physalis* spp.), and cattails (*Typha latifolia*) were either eaten, made into tea, or used medicinally or as dyes. They could be wild collected when stands grew nearby or harvested in cultivated fields if they happened to colonize there.

Prickly pear (*Opuntia* spp.) and claret cup cactus (*Echinocereus triglochidiatus*), four-wing saltbush (*Atriplex canescens*), three-leaf sumac (*Rhus trilobata*), one-seed juniper (*Juniperus monosperma*), rabbitbrush (*Ericameria nauseosus*), mesquites (*Prosopis* spp.), golden currant (*Ribes aureum*), wild rose (*Rosa woodsii*), joint fir (*Ephedra torreyana*), and wolfberry (*Lycium* spp.) are native shrubs that are often found where ancient people lived and gardened, indicators of the transition from wild foraging to farming. By 1000 BCE, early Puebloans were raising several distinct types

of maize, several squashes and beans, pumpkins, and sunflowers. Camp followers that grew in the fields included *Amaranthus* species lamb's quarters and goosefoot, both *Chenopodium* species, purslane (*Portulaca oleracea*), and groundcherry (*Physalis* spp.). Many modern farmers consider these pioneer plants that colonize disturbed soils to be weeds; herbalists consider them medicine. They were given garden space as gifts of nature. Knowledge of Indigenous medicine has survived in the Pueblos and in mixed-culture *curanderismo*, the practice of traditional healing.

Early Colonial Era, 1540-1680

By the 1540s, when the Coronado expedition arrived looking for Eldorado, the fabled Cities of Gold, there were at least a dozen large Tiguex villages between what are now Isleta and Bernalillo. Well-established Native farmers initially welcomed the foreigners, probably warily given the news from Mexico that traveled with the trade goods. Oral histories, as well as diaries of colonists, record the Tiguex generously sharing food stores with their guests. The encounter is a tale of the clash of two very different cultures. It is an iteration of the colonial ethos of the time, whether the explorers were French, English, Spanish, or Portuguese, that "new worlds" were there for the taking. Native subsistence farmers viewed the land as sacred shared spaces and water as life itself, while Spaniards came from a culture that viewed land, water, and people as resources to exploit. There was bound to be trouble. Goodwill ran out as quickly as did the food reserves, and the early Puebloans, without comparable weaponry and despite great loss of life, were temporarily rid of colonial depredation as Coronado moved on seeking the mother lode.

Well before the arrogant despoiling of the Tiguex, the abuse and enslavement of New World Natives by Spanish explorers were reported back to Spain. This so disgusted European human rights activists of the day that by 1535 their outcries compelled King Carlos I to demand: "The murder, plundering and other improper acts that have been done in the said conquest, as well as capturing the Indians as slaves, should cease." In 1537 Pope Paul III, in a papal encyclical, declared that Indians were to be treated humanely and underscored the ban on their enslavement. When Coronado eventually returned to Mexico licking his wounds, he was tried for war crimes, and although stripped of much of his power and wealth, he was eventually acquitted. His shame was his inability to return from the expedition with riches. Coronado's conquistador days were over. The exploitation, however, continued, in many cases by priests who were sent to convert Native souls. If this sounds eerily familiar to our twenty-first century ears, it could just be because then and now people are people in all their diverse and sometimes perverse ways.

In the middle Rio Grande Valley, pragmatic and less brutal Spanish colonists must have recognized an opportunity more life sustaining than the pipe dreams of Eldorado. Many had come to make better lives for themselves and their families, having left nothing behind even if they had been able to return to Mexico or Spain. Like immigrants throughout history, many were driven by desperation and hoped for opportunity earned with sweat equity. By the late 1600s there were a few fortified haciendas where families were grazing cattle, horses, sheep, and goats, ranching as well adapted to the Southwest as it was to Spain. According to letters of Fray Alonso Benavides, a Franciscan provincial custodian in New Mexico in the early 1600s, settlers raised chickens and were growing grapes for winemaking; wheat from Castille; plums, peaches, lentils, chickpeas, watermelons, cantaloupes, cucumbers, lettuces, cabbage, carrots, garlic, onions, and artichokes; and Mexican chiles in addition to the squash, maize, beans, and turkeys that Native farmers traditionally semidomesticated. Enslaved and dragooned Native people provided much of the labor. With the introduction of livestock and the expansion of farming, the demand for water increased. Early Puebloans had long diverted water from springs, arroyos, and lesser tributaries in an early form of channeled irrigation, but the acequias, formalized irrigation technology of Moorish origins that Spaniards brought with them from the Old World, diverted and redistributed Rio Grande waters in a more extensive and somewhat more predictable way.

The cold winter climate of the middle Rio Grande watershed allowed the cultivation of winter wheat (*Triticum aestivum*) and was a boon to the Spanish, both as a source of bread flour and for making sacramental wafers. It was also a way to keep the Puebloans occupied during what the Spanish perceived as downtime, a way to teach their "servants" European diligence. Native peoples traditionally used winter to hunt, to perform ceremonies that reaffirmed their relationship with nature, and to retell stories that strengthened and confirmed cultural identity. Wheat was another wedge between two cultures that differed so fundamentally in worldview. Wheat was also a crop that sustained colonists and Natives alike during the Little Ice Age, a period from the mid-1400s into the early 1800s when intermittently abnormally cold winter temperatures shortened the growing season and limited the ripening of corn crops. Despite more diverse crops and more consistent water, forced labor, the encomienda system of Native labor traded for a patron's protection, introduced diseases, and starvation as colonists appropriated Native crops when their own fell short all took a tremendous toll on the Tiguex, and in 1680 they joined in the Pueblo Revolt, freeing survivors from colonial oppression for less than a generation before the next wave of colonists arrived.

Reconquest and Spanish Colonial Culture, 1681–1821

Only the adaptable can survive and sometimes prosper in such a harsh land, even in the relative abundance of the Rio Grande Valley. For the next two centuries, Natives and colonists managed to persist and grow together. Acequia irrigation further expanded and altered land use patterns. The Spanish allotted long narrow strips to allow each family farm access to water. Upland grazing was shared by individual or community land grants. While crops and acequia irrigation were often adopted by Pueblo people, they maintained their ethos of water as a shared gift and land as not something to own but as a place to belong to and care for, grateful for the life it would provide. Despite renewed ill treatment, early Puebloans did not rise up to repel the reconquest because without the interventions

of the armed Spaniards, they were more vulnerable to the newly emigrated and marauding Navajos, Apaches, and Comanches, who, recently equipped with horses, quickly adapted to the advantages of the equestrian lifestyle. The cultural rift in this case was between settled farming and nomadic survival enhanced by raiding.

During the colonial era, missionaries introduced many different cultivars of fruit trees, which joined the native honey mesquite (*Prosopis glandulosa*), net leaf hackberry (*Celtis reticulata*), chokecherry (*Prunus virginiana* var. *melanocarpa*), and oak (*Quercus* spp.) adopted from early Pueblo people. Crop diversity is food security, and food security can engender tolerance. It was also helpful that although the Christianity being forced upon the Puebloans was for the most part undesirable, some of the major celebrations were related to cycles in nature: the winter solstice, the return of light to the earth, is near Christmas, the birth of the Christian son of God; the spring equinox and the stirring of new life after winter's rest translate easily to Easter, the Christian celebration of the resurrection. The mythology differed, but the basis in natural cycles was similar, so Native rituals could be maintained in the adaptive guise of Christianity.

In 1706 the Villa de Albuquerque was founded, and by 1790 the Spanish census recorded six settlements north of Albuquerque linked by the Camino Real, the trade route from Chihuahua to Santa Fe. Among the settlements were Los Poblanos and Los Ranchos. The place that is Los Poblanos Inn and Organic Farm today was part of the Elena Gallegos de Gurule Land Grant, which covered thirty-five thousand acres extending from the Rio Grande to the crest of the Sandia Mountains, inherited by her son Antonio Gurule upon her death in 1731 and further subdivided among heirs upon his death. The land near the Rio Grande, a five hundred–acre

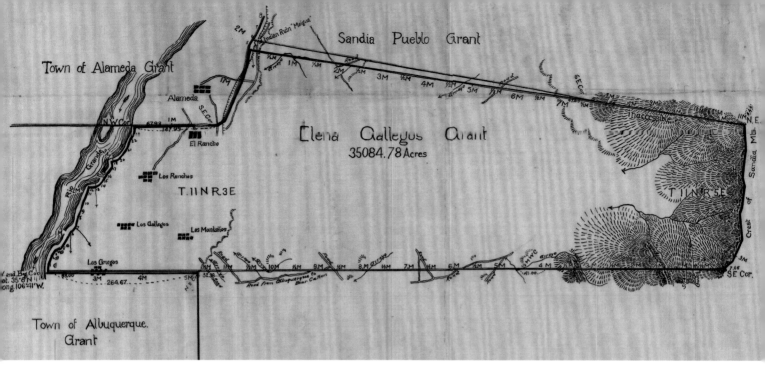

Map of the Elena Gallegos Land Grant. This historic land area was granted to Diego Montoya in 1694, reis-sued to Elena Gallegos in 1712, and over generations subdivided and later sold off by her descendants. The original grant extended west to east from the Rio Grande to the crest of the Sandia Mountains and north to south from present-day Alameda Boulevard almost to Montgomery Boulevard/Montano Road in Albu-querque. Through many land purchases over several years, Albert Gallatin Simms pieced together more than thirty-four thousand acres of the original grant as Los Poblanos Ranch and later disbursed much of it to enrich the Albuquerque Academy endowment. This map is the work of George H. Pradt. Center for Southwest Research, Zimmerman Library, University of New Mexico.

ranch, was purchased by Ambrosio and Cristobal Armijo in the early 1800s. San Antonio de Los Pobla-nos is first recorded as a community of twenty-three people in the 1802 census; the name of the ranch and the early village is thought to refer to settlers who emigrated from Puebla, Mexico. The Simms Los Poblanos Ranch gradually grew to reunite much of the Elena Gallegos Land Grant before constricting back to its present twenty-five acres of what may have been the original Armijo ranch.

Mexican and Territorial Period, 1821-1912

Mexico declared independence from Spain in 1821, and New Mexico was claimed as a territory of the United States in 1846, but statehood was still a long time in coming. New Mexico was too foreign a land in climate, terrain, and cultures for eastern lawmakers to easily embrace. What had originally been seventy to one hundred independent Native communities was reduced by Spanish colonial-ism to the current nineteen pueblos, the Navajo Nation (Diné), and the Jicarilla, Mescalero, and other Apache groups. Mexico granted citizenship to all Native peoples, so New Mexico's first peoples became citizens of the United States by default at the end of the US war with Mexico. (Most of the other southwestern Natives were delayed citizen-ship until the Indian Citizenship Act of 1924, years after many Native warriors fought for the United States in the First World War.) In 1864 President

Abraham Lincoln awarded silver-tipped, inscribed governor's canes to the nineteen New Mexican pueblos, recognizing them as sovereign nations. Although national politics had less of an impact on the land than human exploitation did in this brittle ecology, Lincoln's acknowledgment has had a profound impact on water rights along the Rio Grande into modern times. Native people's priority right to water is law, even as land use has evolved and continues to shape decisions made at the gardens at Los Poblanos.

Josiah Gregg, explorer, naturalist, and trader, wrote in *The Journal of a Santa Fe Trader* in 1844, "When these regions were first discovered it appears that the inhabitants lived in comfortable houses and cultivated the soil, as they have continued to do up to the present time. Indeed, they are now considered the best horticulturists in the country, furnishing most of the fruits and a large portion of the vegetable supplies that are to be found in the markets. They are, in short, a remarkably sober and industrious race, conspicuous for morality and honesty, and very little given to quarreling or dissipation." While complimenting Indigenous farmers who continued to feed the increasing tide of interlopers, Gregg did not distinguish Natives by culture and language, unintentionally reinforcing the imperialist erasure of the multiplicity of local cultures.

As the human population grew, water used for irrigation in the middle Rio Grande Valley continued to increase over time. The 40,185 acres irrigated in 1850 swelled to 54,500 acres in 1860. By 1870, 4,480 farms, 85 percent of them less than fifty acres, were irrigating 143,000 acres, but ten years later irrigated acreage had dropped to ninety-five thousand acres. Corn, wheat, and beans were supplemented with oats, barley, sorghum and rye grains and peas, potatoes, tobacco, and alfalfa hay. After the death of Juan Cristobal Armijo in 1884, Los Poblanos

Ranch lands were divided among his many descendants and parceled into many small subsistence family farms. By 1894 colonists of yet another race, the first Russian thistle—tumbleweed (*Salsola tragus*), thought to have been introduced in imported flaxseed—had taken root in New Mexico. The end of the nineteenth century saw subsistence farmers in the Los Poblanos area struggling with a strangely erratic river carrying much heavier silt loads that raised the level of the riverbed and left standing water where there had been productive farmland. The times, the land, and the river were changing.

The cottonwood forest was cut for fuel and lumber, and many of the upper watershed conifers had been clear-cut to build the railroad in the 1880s. The railroad then brought in cattle and sheep of wealthy absentee landowners, who viewed land as a commodity to exploit and accelerated the overgrazing encouraged by improved shipping access to midwestern and eastern markets. Ecologically productive grasslands were reduced to what some saw as desert wasteland, and the denuded slopes in the upper watershed contributed tons of sediment, which was deposited by flash flooding into the Rio Abajo, the lower watershed. Akin to barn doors and escaped horses, in 1889 the General Land Office began requiring ranchers to obtain permits to graze on New Mexico's public lands. Still, many farmers in the valley were unaware of the connection between overgrazing and the increasing unpredictability of the flows of the Rio Grande.

In addition to deforestation and the resulting flooding, the 1880s arrival of the railroad brought development to New Town Albuquerque, new settlers, and new employment in railroad maintenance, sawmills, a brick factory, and a wool scouring mill just north of the new downtown. By 1908 the American Lumber Company, north of Old Town, employed more than one thousand men.

Rio Grande flood, 1920. Clear–cutting of forests and grazing in the Sangre de Cristo and Jemez Mountains increased sediment loads in the many tributaries that drain into the Rio Grande, making the river more and more unpredictable. Thus flooding became a too common plight in the Rio Grande Valleys. The Middle Rio Grande Conservancy District and later the Albuquerque Municipal Flood Control Authority were created to address the unintended consequences of development. PA1992.005.064, Albuquerque Museum purchase.

The younger generation, seeing more secure livelihoods as industrial laborers, abandoned farming except as small-scale gardeners putting food on their families' tables or moonlighting as seasonal help for relatives still making their living from the land. Lumber mills, brick manufacturing, and rail-delivered tin roofing fostered the shift from traditional soft-edged, flat-roofed adobe buildings—the mud huts scorned by newcomers—to brick and wood frame construction. Buildings with sharp corners, milled lumber trim around doors and windows, brick coping along rooflines, and pitched roofs clad in tin made New Town Albuquerque look more like home to eastern eyes.

What had been a largely barter economy rapidly shifted to a cash one, and catering to "foreign" tastes may have expedited New Mexico's path to statehood in 1912. Wealth-seeking newcomers and old Hispanic families intent on holding their own in changing times tried to minimize the cultural differences inherent in the genetically diverse population, whitewashing the rainbow of skin tones and ideals that made New Mexico such a vital place. Ironically, at the same time, Fred Harvey and the Atchison, Topeka and Santa Fe Railway were marketing exotic southwestern triculturalism, pure air, and sunshine and were building their restaurants, hotels, and depots in imitation of traditional architecture. That ambivalence prevails to this day, as people who exclaim at the beauty of the desert landscape would still rather look at it from a distance than live in it on its own terms.

Exotic plant introductions extended into the landscape with the federal government promoting farming and ranching with "use it or lose it" water laws at the same time younger New Mexicans were seeking their livelihoods in New Town. The railroad made shipping exotic plants to farms and gardens in the West feasible. The first tree nursery in New Mexico opened in Santa Fe in 1868. J. Blaisdell, a nurseryman from Rochester, New York, took orders for plants to be shipped to customers. Archbishop Jean Baptiste Lamy was developing extensive gardens on the cathedral grounds and encouraging Santa Feans to garden their city. Newer selections of apples and pears, shade and ornamental trees such as elms (*Ulmus* spp.), the horse chestnut *Aesculus hippocastanatum*, and the black locust *Robinia pseudoacacia* began displacing previously grown native cottonwoods (*Populus deltoides* spp. *wislizeni*), oaks (*Quercus* spp.), Arizona sycamores (*Platanus wrightii*) and velvet ash (*Fraxinus velutina*).

Since the early 1800s, the Jeffersonian "cult of the exotic" has been a well-intentioned endeavor to improve American landscapes by introducing plants from all over the globe to bolster the agricultural economy. "The greatest service which can be rendered any country is to add a useful plant to its culture," Thomas Jefferson said. While that is proving to be ecologically short-sighted, we have certainly reaped the culinary benefit. Nonnative food crops are now 98 percent of total US food production. In the Rio Grande watershed, foreign food crops, many established here centuries ago, are so much a delicious part of our diets and cultures that we scarcely think of them as alien. It is only when exotic plants disrupt the stability and structure of native plant communities and the wildlife that they support that they are labeled noxious weeds to be eradicated. The term *ecology* was not coined until 1866, forty years after Jefferson's death.

Plants such as Russian olive (*Elaeagnus angustifolia*) and salt cedar (*Tamarix chinensis*) were introduced as ornamentals and for erosion control. Siberian elms (*Ulmus pumila*) were given away by the tens of thousands to provide valuable shade. Merely controlling the spread of these plants, once seen as useful innovations, is now a daunting prospect. Our relationship with plants changes with our understanding of their attributes. Much like marriages ending in divorce, the romance that focused on shining virtues yields to the realities of living with the vices. Our realization of what exotics cost in damage to local ecology is only now beginning to hit home. The role that displacing native plants with exotic ornamentals plays in declines in songbird and pollinator populations is only now being documented as a contributing factor, along with pesticide use and climate shifts, to the cascades of extinction we are now witnessing.

By the 1880s, in larger towns across New Mexico, agents from eastern nurseries began taking orders for edible and ornamental plants from farmers and city folks alike plants to be shipped bare-root in spring by rail. Across the country, the 1887 Hatch Act led to the establishment of agricultural experiment stations to test newly introduced exotics. Soon after, in 1889, the New Mexico College of Agriculture and Mechanical Arts in Las Cruces was designated as a land grant school. Part of its mission was to assess the adaptability and productivity of exotics in New Mexico's harsh climate. Those mandates are still being addressed at its successor institution, New Mexico State University, along with the realization of how the land grant universities were developed on lands once again appropriated from Native peoples.

By the early 1900s, Albuquerque had urbanized to the extent that civic beautification organizations and horticultural societies advocated the importation of exotic ornamentals. The City Beautiful movement was a collaboration between architects, landscape architects, and urban planners bolstered by the World's Columbian Exposition in 1893. In America's rapidly urbanizing areas, City Beautiful was a reform philosophy seeking to promote order, harmony, and civic loyalty through improved sanitation, safer circulation of traffic, and monumental structures, parks, and public spaces. European beaux arts design was the model. Nationwide, the cult of the lawn, with carpet-bedding annuals as accents, had become the residential landscape norm in formal street-facing gardens. Backyards were given over to kitchen gardens to feed the household. The majority of people still had a connection to plants through food.

Simultaneously, the Country Place era (1870 to the 1930s) in American landscape architecture had begun, with somewhat divergent trends. The style draws its rejoicing in nature and its combi-nation of agriculture and ornament from Roman villas, which evolved over centuries into the Italian Renaissance style, with garden rooms, walled and hedged spaces, and the sensory experience of running water, birdsong, and fragrant planting. While the Country Place era in America embraced European-derived beaux arts formality and opulence indulged in by the wealthy, the formality was tempered by the international arts and crafts movement, an everyman's philosophical reaction to industrialization. Respect for precapitalist artisan craftsmanship was seen as a means of positive social reform, and a few utopian communities were founded in the eastern United States. The arts and crafts movement also promoted regionalism in the landscape, advocating the use of native plants. International trends trickled west slowly. New Mexico, despite centuries-long pressure to homogenize, was still steeped in traditional cultures, and the difficult climate made working within native plant communities the path of least resistance. Yet even in New Mexico, change was in the wind.

New Mexico's Statehood and Taming the Rio Grande, 1913-1950

As New Town Albuquerque developed, builders embraced many architectural styles, including folk Victorian, Queen Anne, Gothic revival, and Mediterranean revival, as well as our own Pueblo revival, territorial revival, and mission revival. The English garden influence of manicured lawns, massed shrubs, perennial beds, and foundation planting surrounded the diverse architecture. Traditional adobe homes had no basements, so there was no practical need to screen stem walls, with the exception of wood frame and brick houses in New Town built with basements, so novelty and style prevailed and foundation planting became the vogue.

Acequia-flooded lawns helped keep the dust down and offered some summertime cooling, and exotic plants poorly adapted to an arid climate continued to increase water use.

As the city grew and the floodplain of the Rio Grande through Albuquerque became more populated, damage from repeated flooding increased. While there were new markets for farm goods, there were fewer young farmers working fewer acres as the valley became increasingly swamped by rising water tables and frequent flooding. In 1923 the New Mexico State Legislature created the Middle Rio Grande Conservancy District (MRGCD). Its staff, working with the Army Corps of Engineers, channelized the Rio Grande to stop flooding and reclaim land for farming. Drainage ditches were dug to reclaim marshland, and the oldest local acequias were absorbed into a regional system. Cottonwoods returned to MRGCD levees and were preserved along acequias built to distribute irrigation water through the valley and to mitigate flooding—certainly progress in many eyes. According to the 1980 Los Poblanos District National Register of Historic Places inventory nomination form, the Griegos Lateral, a major acequia that forms the western boundary of the present-day gardens of Los Poblanos, is "among the ditches that show up on the earliest maps of the north valley and the individual ditches it feeds may be of comparable age. The acequia network accounts for the richness of the district's landscapes, making plenitude of water available in the dry Albuquerque climate; the network is also one of the chief beauties of the district with water running spring to fall through the tree and reed-bordered ditches."

Not everyone benefited equally from the taming of the Rio Grande. Traditional subsistence farmers shared and bartered goods apart from the

Griegos Lateral, shown here in 2021, is one of the oldest acequias in Albuquerque and is the west boundary of Los Poblanos. Looking north, this is the middle gate of the three acequias into Los Poblanos. The acequias are no longer the sole water source for local farmers but are critical for maintaining the connection between the shallow aquifer and the Rio Grande throughout the basin. The tree-lined acequias have become an important community green space, maintaining the lush, rural appeal of the valley. Photograph by the author.

cash economy. The added tax burden on what had been water earned by community participation to maintain the acequias caused more cultural upheaval as small farms were lost to foreclosure. Adding more pressure, the tax bills for flood control improvements began just as the Great Depression drained away meager financial security. As Jorge Garcia, senior program manager of El Centro de la Raza, Division of Student Affairs at the University of New Mexico, explained at the 2021 Land and Water Summit in Albuquerque, "The 1920s–1930s were a very difficult time for acequias in the middle Rio Grande. The creation of the Middle Rio Grande Conservancy District was the right thing to do to support the delivery and management of water, as well as the draining of the valley. Even though the creation of the MRGCD was a support to the infrastructure, the locals viewed it as a takeover by the US government and a dismantling of a local custom and system of governance, and instead of being a positive step, it became a negative aspect that moved on with time."

Dairy farms prospered as the city grew. By 1920 there were nearly one hundred licensed dairies in the valley, mostly small family businesses that eventually formed the Albuquerque Cooperative Dairy Association to process and deliver valley-produced milk. Local farmers and investors, including Albert and Ruth Simms, purchased a production facility on Second Street north of downtown in 1937 and renamed the cooperative Creamland Dairies. Los Poblanos Ranch, the largest contributor to the co-op, was active in the transition and moved local agriculture a step further toward larger farms as business ventures. The Simmses' comparative wealth set them apart from many small local farmers and ranchers, however, Albert and Ruth were investors and also hands-on participants, active in the community and in agriculture specifically. Matt Rembe, Los Poblanos's present CEO, recalls Sam King, partner with his family in King Brothers' Alamo Ranch, describing the first corn harvester in New Mexico. Albert Simms introduced it to his fellow farmers in the valley, inviting them to the ranch to try it out. Sharing new technology and ideas was part of the culture of Los Poblanos from the very beginning.

Between 1932 and 1938, New Mexico, Colorado, and Texas negotiated the Rio Grande Compact to apportion water among the states. The unintended consequences of human activities were gaining momentum, with river-borne sediment in the middle Rio Grande floodplain accumulating by about a foot a year from 1936 into the 1940s. At the same time, the US Soil Conservation Service was established to deal with Dust Bowl erosion. It recommended that marginal farmland be returned to native grassland—easier said than done in arid landscapes. The MRGCD drained the wetlands,

and once the marshes were reclaimed, the valley flourished. At the end of World War II, there were sixty thousand acres of irrigated farmland along the Rio Grande in the Albuquerque area. More than half of the forty-seven hundred farms had fewer than 15 acres; 44 percent of the rest had 16 to 160 or more acres. Cultivating alfalfa (*Medicago sativa*) pastures for grazing and hay allowed farmers to work away from the farm and still profit from their land. Subdivisions boomed along Edith Boulevard and North Second and Fourth Streets while larger estates developed along Rio Grande Boulevard, closer to the Rio itself.

Suburbanization and Albuquerque's North Valley Landscapes, 1950-2021

Until the late 1950s, much of the Southwest suffered a severe, prolonged drought, which ended in part with a March 1955 blizzard that left ten-foot snowdrifts in its wake. To usher the always erratic climate of New Mexico into modern times, the end of that 1950s drought period began a thirty-year wet anomaly in precipitation compared with the previous one thousand years, with fairly consistent snowpack in the mountains and regular monsoon rainfall. This climatic grace period coincided with Albuquerque's largest building boom, which in part occurred to accommodate the growing number of employees of Sandia National Laboratory and the University of New Mexico. Suburbs sprouted up on the mesas and in the valley, encroaching on traditional farms and ranchland. Lawns, shade trees, and rose bushes replaced rangeland, orchards, and vegetable fields. The new homeowners assumed that the generous precipitation was normal. Certainly, the shade trees planted during the wet years benefited from the relative abundance of moisture, establishing the extensive roots they need to cope with otherwise less than ideal growing conditions.

The increase in hard surfaces, pavements, and rooftops and the soil compaction that results from the use of heavy machinery to mass-grade subdivisions covering what had been permeable soil led to flooding in the newly urbanized areas, and in 1963 the Albuquerque Municipal Flood Control Authority was created to manage urban storm water. Many of the arroyos were channelized and paved to protect property in flood-prone areas and to drain storm water to the river as directly and swiftly as possible. Engineering and irrigation technology made building in marginal areas and maintaining plantings that required double and triple the natural rainfall possible if not sustainable. Business boosters had floated the fantasy that Albuquerque sat on an aquifer comparable to Lake Superior, but by the early 1990s, water resources had begun showing signs of stress. Groundwater levels in some of the city's wells dropped precipitously enough to raise a concern about land subsidence, a threat to real estate that could not be blamed on "acts of God." Water conservation measures were initiated to protect groundwater levels and *xeriscape* became an often-misunderstood term for water-conservative landscaping.

In common parlance, *xeriscape* became *zeroscape*. Plants were replaced with sheets of gravel that raised the ambient temperature and undermined shade trees that had been part of the green cooling of the city. For several decades, great efforts were made to educate the public about the benefits of native and other climate-adapted plants. The Xeriscape Council of New Mexico, founded in the early 1980s, held tours of well-designed xeric landscapes and hosted conferences and expos, attempting to dispel the simplistic notion that xeriscapes

were gravelscapes. Because half or more of the water used per capita is used outdoors on irrigation, the Albuquerque Bernalillo County Water Utility Authority published xeriscape guides, with photos of colorful xeric plants and information on how to grow them. Books demonstrated the diversity and beauty of native and arid-adapted plants. Many people heard the message and converted their lawns to colorful, fragrant, wildlife-friendly gardens. In 1995 per capita water use in Albuquerque was 251 gallons per day. By 2015 per capita use had dropped to 127 gallons per day.

The Xeriscape Council of New Mexico gradually began to distance itself from the misunderstood term. What had been called xeriscape or water conservation conferences were rebranded as land and water summits focused on the importance of healthy soils, storm water as a valuable natural resource, and plants as critical components of urban ecology. In 2018 the Xeriscape Council finally rebranded the water-conserving garden concept as "resiliency in Southwest landscapes" to link water and land use with pollinator and wildlife support. At the same time, the Friends of Albuquerque's new national wildlife refuge, Valle de Oro, began the Albuquerque Backyard Refuge Program to encourage homeowners to plant native plants in their gardens to support wildlife, songbirds, and pollinators. Conservation isn't about sacrificing the good things in life; it's about making resources go further in sustaining life.

Finding apt labels for complex concepts is difficult. Promoters of ecologically sound landscaping found *xeriscape* to be too narrow a label for the practice of designing for rapidly changing climate and support of wildlife that makes ecosystems whole and functional within a sustainable water budget. Some landscape architects in the United States and abroad have also found the label *land-*

scape architecture to be too narrow to describe a discipline that is both art and science. Designing resilient landscapes capable of adapting to change yet serving current needs is a complex and ideally collaborative endeavor informed by archaeology, ecology, history, forestry, planning, agronomy, psychology, civil engineering, sociology, and hydrology. Is it any wonder that many people have no idea what a landscape architect does?

Because of access to acequia water and the ease of drilling shallow irrigation wells in the valley, landscapes along the Rio Grande remained lush and green. Alfalfa became a small landholder's best option for a crop that could be grown profitably while the landholder worked full-time at another job. Although alfalfa is fairly thirsty, flooded alfalfa fields help maintain the shallow aquifer, are a nectar source for leaf-cutting bees, and improve the soil by breaking up compaction with deep, nitrogen-fixing roots.

Unfortunately, managing acequia irrigation became out of step with the pace of modern lifestyles, and much contemporary lawn grass is irrigated with sprinklers, the least efficient way to apply water because so much is lost to evaporation in the dry air. The flood irrigation that recycles water back to the shallow aquifer has kept much of the cottonwood canopy healthy. But pumping from shallow wells that supply sprinkler irrigation has gradually dropped the water table below existing tree root zones, hastening the decline of the aging North Valley tree canopy. The idea that shallow wells do not have an impact on valley ecology—that is, "We're not using city water; we have a well"—ignores the reality that all the straws are drinking from the same glass.

The village of Los Ranchos, which surrounds Los Poblanos Inn and Organic Farm, was incorporated at the end of 1958 to protect one of the last remaining rural expanses in the valley from the suburban expansion of Albuquerque. Land use and lot size restrictions have preserved the agricultural feel and kept land values elevated to the extent that descendants of some of the early settlers and post-WWII boomers struggle to maintain their properties. Los Poblanos has remained true to the cultural values of this place, maintaining acequia irrigation where feasible as well as continuing the agricultural mandate more efficiently by drip-irrigating lavender (*Lavandula* × *intermedia* 'Grosso'), a water-conservative crop of high value for the water invested. Squash, beans, maize, asparagus, greens, tomatoes, and other food crops continue to supply Campo, the inn's restaurant. The historic gardens at Los Poblanos grow along with native and other arid-adapted plants. The historic tree canopy is carefully tended while new planting of less water-intensive species maintains the lush green mixed with contrasting silvers and sage.

Today the multilayered cultures in the Rio Grande Basin live and work together companionably for the most part, but old wounds still throb just below the mostly calm veneer. DNA testing of New Mexicans is revealing that we are far from pure genetically; we are all hybrids and richer for it. On her website, historian Alicia Inez Guzman suggests that we explore and embrace the complexity of who we really are in order to right the myth of a tricultural New Mexico—Native, Hispanic, Anglo—and the one-dimensional ideas implied by conquest and imperialism. She proposes that being unsettled by our history in this place is the path to empathy and a kinder, more generous future.

Food and art are common and essential to human nature. Plants—whether for food, medicine, dyes, building material, or sheer beauty—have always been a shared interest between people.

Rio Grande, June 2021. Without bountiful mountain snow in winter and after valley farmers have begun to irrigate, the Rio is reduced to braided streams meandering across the broader riverbed. Photograph by Hunter Ten Broeck.

Small-scale local artisan farms are in many ways a bridge between industrial agriculture and the ethos of Indigenous peoples' identification with the land and the ecology that keeps it whole. Still and always, gardening here is the gift of the Rio Grande's water. Feeding people locally and restoring habitat for wildlife by returning native plants to the land as a means of creating beautiful, resilient landscapes for people to relax in and enjoy are ways to manage water wisely for future generations of gardeners. The story of the gardens of Los Poblanos past and present is a saga of culture and change,

adaptability, and resilience. New chapters continue to be written here and hopefully always will be.

Sources, and an Invitation to Dig Deeper

Albuquerque Bernalillo County Water Utility Authority. "Xeriscape for a Desert-Friendly Yard." ABCWUA, 2021, https://www.abcwua.org/conservation-rebates-xeriscape.

Cajete, Gregory, ed. *A People's Ecology: Explora-*

tions in Sustainable Living. Santa Fe: Clear Light, 1999.

Clark, Ira G. Water in New Mexico: A History of Its Management and Use. Albuquerque: University of New Mexico Press, 1987.

Coan, Charles F. A History of New Mexico. Chicago: American Historical Society, 1925.

Davis, Brian, and Thomas Oles. "From Architecture to Landscape." Places, October 2014, https://placesjournal.org/article/from-architecture-to-landscape.

Dunmire, William W. Gardens of New Spain: How Mediterranean Plants and Foods Changed America. Austin: University of Texas Press, 2004.

Dunmire, William W., and Gail D. Tierney. Wild Plants of the Pueblo Province: Exploring Ancient and Enduring Uses. Santa Fe: Museum of New Mexico Press, 1995.

505 Outside. "Current Watering Recommendations." 505 Outside, https://www.505outside.com/, accessed October 25, 2022.

Flint, Richard. Great Cruelties Have Been Reported: The 1544 Investigation of the Coronado Expedition. Dallas: Southern Methodist University Press, 2002.

Friends of Valle de Oro National Wildlife Refuge. "ABQ Backyard Refuge Program." Friends of Valle de Oro National Wildlife Refuge, https://friendsofvalledeoro.org/abq-backyard-refuge, accessed October 25, 2022.

Gutzler, David S., and Sarah J. Keller. "Observed Trends in Snowpack and Spring Season Soil Moisture Affecting New Mexico." New Mexico Journal of Science 46, no. 1 (2012):169–81.

Hall, Edward T. West of the Thirties: Discoveries among the Navajo and Hopi. New York: Bantam Doubleday Dell, 1994.

Kaufman, S. R., and W. Kaufman. Invasive Plants: Guide to Identification and the Impacts and Control of Common North American Species. Mechanicsburg, PA: Stackpole Books, 2007.

Lamb, H. H. Climatic History and the Future. Princeton, NJ: Princeton University Press, 1977.

New Mexico Earth Matters. "New Mexico's Changing Climate." New Mexico Earth Matters, 2004, https://geoinfo.nmt.edu/publications/periodicals/earthmatters/4/n2/em_v4_n2.pdf.

New Mexico Genealogical Society. "NMGS DNA Project." NMGS, https://www.nmgs.org/nmgs-dna-project, accessed October 25, 2022.

Martin, Paul S. The Last 10,000 Years: A Fossil Pollen Record of the American Southwest. Tucson: University of Arizona Press, 1963.

Morrow, Baker H., ed. and trans. A Harvest of Reluctant Souls: Fray Alonso de Benavides's History of New Mexico, 1630. Albuquerque: University of New Mexico Press, 1996.

PlantUse. "Nicotiana rustica (PROSEA)." PlantUse, 2016, https://uses.plantnet-project.org/en/Nicotiana_rustica_(PROSEA).

Sabatini, Joe. "Area History." Near North Valley Neighborhood Association, August 14, 2018, https://sites.google.com/site/nearnorthvalleyassociation/home/area-history.

Sando, Joe S. Pueblo Nations: Eight Centuries of Pueblo Indians History. Santa Fe: Clear Light, 1992.

Sargeant, Kathryn, and Mary Davis. Shining River, Precious Land: An Oral History of Albuquerque's North Valley. Albuquerque: Albuquerque Museum, 1986.

Scurlock, Dan. *From the Rio to the Sierra: An Environmental History of the Middle Rio Grande Basin*. US Forest Service, US Department of Agriculture, 1998, https://www.fs.usda.gov/treesearch/pubs/5133.

Swan, Linda Susan. "Climate, Crops and Livestock: Some Aspects of Mexican Agriculture." PhD diss., Washington State University, 1977.

Tallamy, Douglas W. *Nature's Best Hope: A New Approach to Conservation That Starts in Your Yard*. Portland, OR: Timber Press, 2019.

Underhill, Ruth. *Life in the Pueblos*. Santa Fe: Ancient City Press, 1991.

Van Citters, Karen. *A Brief History of Urban Trees in New Mexico*. Groundwork Studio, January 15, 2018, https://groundworkstudionm.com/wp-content/uploads/2019/06/A-Brief-History-of-Urban-Trees-in-NM.pdf.

CHAPTER 2

The Country Place Era of American Landscapes

> Landscape is history made visible.
>
> —J. B. Jackson, essayist and cultural geographer

Linked to horticulture and agriculture, landscape architecture is a relatively new art and science in the United States. Michigan State University was the first to award a degree in landscape architecture, in 1898. Design-wise, the discipline in America was heavily influenced by European traditions. To understand the American adaptation of mostly European landscape styles in the New World, it is valuable to examine the roots of ornamental garden practices, starting with ancient Persian pleasure gardens that, over millennia, evolved into the Italian Renaissance villa landscapes admired by wealthy Americans while traveling abroad.

The earliest archaeological record of ornamental gardens dates to circa 4000 BCE in Mesopotamia. By 500 BCE, Persian garden style was well developed and widespread. Wall-enclosed spaces were divided into four quadrants by water channels, which likely had symbolic significance as well

as the practical job of delivering irrigation water. Lapis-tiled geometric fountains provided humidity and cooling. The quadrants were planted with the Asian plane tree (*Platanus orientalis*), mulberries (*Morus* spp.), figs (*Ficus carica*), date palms (*Phoenix dactylifera*), and trellised grapevines. *Vitis* species provided both shade and food, while roses (*Rosa* spp.) perfumed the air. Persian garden influences still color landscape design today, especially in the southwestern United States, where the climate extremes are similar to those of the arid eastern Mediterranean.

In climates that were uncomfortably hot and dry, and that at higher elevations could be seasonally frigid, Persian paradise gardens fulfilled basic physical and spiritual needs. The design concepts spread across the Middle East and North Africa, into Greece and Italy, and eventually to Spain, adapting to the local cultures, traditions, and ecology. By 100 BCE, Roman landscape style, evolving from garden practices that came before, was blossoming. As the Roman Empire expanded, Roman garden design became a widespread influence across Europe and eventually in America's Country Place gardens.

While plebeian Romans grew gardens on a small scale as sources of food as well as places of respite, the remains of the villas of the wealthy and the writings of the learned are sources of much of the information available today. According to Pliny the Younger, circa 100 CE, villas were generally located on high ground to capture the distant views and included courtyard spaces with trellises, colonnades, and pergolas for privacy and protection. The formal axial boundaries of spaces within gardens were set by canals that provided irrigation water, but planting patterns varied greatly and included circular and crescent-shaped beds. Fruit and shade trees lined connecting cross-axial walkways, and fountains and sculptures were foci. Elements were positioned to enhance ventilation, buffer summer sun, filter dust, and facilitate the irrigation necessary to maintain lush planting.

As the power and unity of the Roman Empire declined, monasteries became the repositories of knowledge, including botanical expertise. In monastery gardens, colonnades formed the open sides of cloisters around spaces divided into quadrilateral beds. Central fountains were water sources but also had religious significance, just as they did in Persian times. Medicinal herbs; sacred plants such as bay (*Laurus nobilis*), holly (*Ilex aquifolium*), yew (*Taxus* spp.), hazel (*Corylus avellana*), mulberry (*Morus alba*), roses (*Rosa gallica officinalis*), and lily (*Lilium candidum*); sage (*Salvia officinalis*), clary sage (*Salvia sclarea*), boneset (*Symphytum officinale*), rue (*Ruta graveolens*), and lavender (*Lavandula angustifolia*) perfumed the beds and were used to heal the sick. Orchards, vineyards, and vegetable gardens were typically protected by substantial walls.

In the thirteenth century, Renaissance Italy saw a rebirth in garden design inspired by the classical ideals of beauty and order. Lavish gardens were financed by the wealth and power of the church and by merchant bankers, notably the Medici family. These gardens were associated with palatial villas, where ideally the dwelling occupied a hilltop and formal gardens were laid out on terraces down the slope. The most intricate plantings were located where they could be enjoyed from windows and doorways. Axial geometry and symmetry imposed control over nature. Sculpture and fountains, grand promenades, secluded garden rooms, and topiary planting were based on newly rediscovered ancient Roman villa garden descriptions. Italian Renaissance style spread throughout Europe.

Early American Landscape Design: Key Developments and Pioneers

The early 1840s publication of *A Treatise on the Theory and Practice of Landscape Gardening Adapted to North America*, written by Andrew Jackson Downing, could be considered the birth of American landscape design as a discipline. Downing's *Treatise* was adapted from John Louden's *The Landscape Gardening and Landscape Architecture of the Late Humphry Repton, Esq.* Repton, who followed in the footsteps of Capability Brown, had a long and celebrated career improving the estates of the wealthy throughout England. Brown and Repton replaced the formal Renaissance gardens of the seventeenth century with sweeping greenswards, tree groupings, and expansive artificial lakes in more naturalistic compositions.

Downing was perhaps the first American house and garden celebrity. Certainly he was one of the most notable plantsmen of the time. He favored simple, natural, and perennial over ornate, artificial, and ephemeral planting schemes and promoted the *ferme ornee* concept of the ornamental and working farm, where the pleasure garden, kitchen garden, and surrounding farmland were parts of a coherent whole. Thomas Jefferson's gardens at Monticello are a notable example. A contemporary of Emerson and Thoreau, Downing viewed restlessness as a part of the American national character and felt that gardens and parks could be "a means to settle people," foreshadowing the City Beautiful movement. Downing's life and career were cut short in a boating accident in 1852, when he was only thirty-six years old, yet he left a legacy that influenced the American-designed landscape well after his death.

As the country industrialized and cities became crowded, polluted, and crime-ridden, the City Beautiful movement sought to promote "order, harmony, and virtue" in urban centers by creating monumental civic architecture, parks, and public spaces. Frederick Law Olmsted, a leading founder of American landscape architecture, who practiced from 1857 to 1895, viewed parks and public green spaces as vehicles for mending societal divides and improving the mental and physical health of all urban citizens. Central Park in New York City, opened in 1859, was one of his first landscape collaborations. Many projects later, Olmstead adapted his plan for Washington and Jackson Park, which was derailed by the Great Chicago Fire in 1871, and for the 1893 Columbian Exposition/Chicago World's Fair and helped launch the City Beautiful movement. Beaux arts style, emulating the European Renaissance, was also popularized at the exposition in Chicago. The style included tree-lined boulevards and allées, grand pavilions, reflecting pools, garden rooms enclosed by sheared hedges, and the use of stone for columns, fountains, walls, and varied and detailed paving.

Charles Platt, a Paris-trained painter, self-taught architect, and landscape architect, traveled to Italy to tour gardens and returned to distill his impressions in *Italian Gardens*, published in 1894. He is credited with introducing the beaux arts style more broadly in the United States. Platt's work combined formal and informal themes and linked houses to gardens both visually and with brick walkways laid out on axes. For plant selection, he often collaborated closely with Warren H. Manning and Ellen Shipman. Manning was a landscape architect and plantsman who had worked with Olmsted. Shipman, one of America's first female landscape architects, had been mentored by Platt. She adopted Platt's style of strong axial relationships between the house and gardens laid out as a series of outdoor rooms. While Manning favored Olmsted's adaptive American vision, balancing formal beaux arts style with immersion in naturalized scenery, Shipman seems to have embraced the formal. But like Manning, she used her knowledge of plants to buffer the artificiality of rigid design.

The Country Place Era

The Country Place era in the United States was a period of estate building by newly wealthy Americans that ran from approximately 1870 to 1930 in the East and Midwest and continued for at least another decade in the Southwest. The beaux arts trend toward rigid formality and ornate decoration was enthusiastically adopted by newly wealthy Americans. Grand estates with lavish gardens surrounding impressive, often monumental architecture included features such as formal terraces, parterres, fountains, and sculpture. All

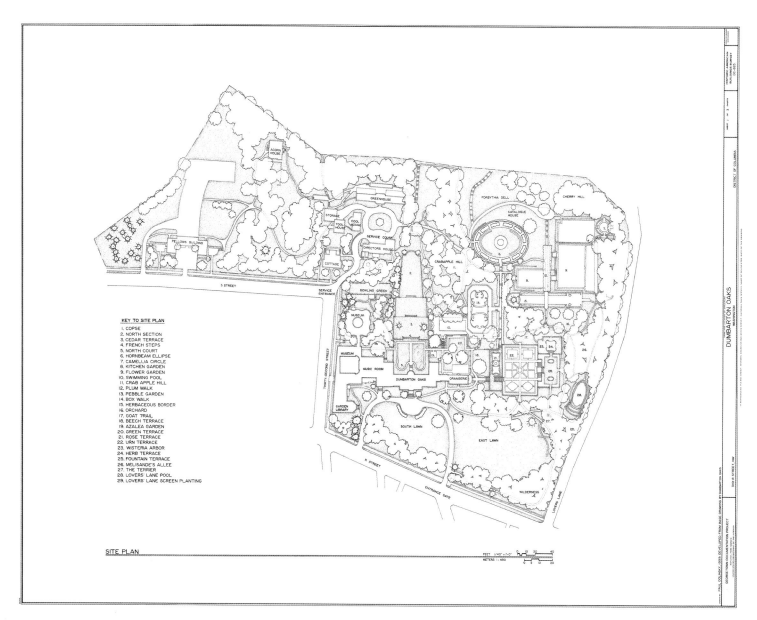

HISTORIC AMERICAN BUILDINGS SURVEY
DC-825
SHEET 1 OF 3 SHEETS
DISTRICT OF COLUMBIA

DUMBARTON OAKS
WASHINGTON

3101 R STREET, NW

KEY TO SITE PLAN
1. COPSE
2. NORTH SECTION
3. CEDAR TERRACE
4. FRENCH STEPS
5. NORTH COURT
6. HORNBEAM ELLIPSE
7. CAMELLIA CIRCLE
8. KITCHEN GARDEN
9. FLOWER GARDEN
10. SWIMMING POOL
11. CRAB APPLE HILL
12. PLUM WALK
13. PEBBLE GARDEN
14. BOX WALK
15. HERBACEOUS BORDER
16. ORCHARD
17. GOAT TRAIL
18. BEECH TERRACE
19. AZALEA GARDEN
20. GREEN TERRACE
21. ROSE TERRACE
22. URN TERRACE
23. WISTERIA ARBOR
24. HERB TERRACE
25. FOUNTAIN TERRACE
26. MELISANDE'S ALLEE
27. THE TERRIER
28. LOVERS' LANE POOL
29. LOVERS' LANE SCREEN PLANTING

SITE PLAN

Dunbarton Oaks garden plan. Darling Archive, Alamy stock photo.

were intended to impress with opulence and give a patina of age and grace to American new money.

Many of these famous gardens—including Biltmore, the Vanderbilt estate in North Carolina, designed by Frederick Law Olmsted; Frank Lloyd Wright's Fallingwater in southwestern Pennsylvania; and Fair Lane, the estate of the Ford family in Dearborn, Michigan, with gardens designed by Jens Jensen—have a modern presence as muse-

ums, cultural centers, and botanic gardens. Since 1993, Chanticleer, near Philadelphia, has been open to the public as a "pleasure garden," It is similar to Los Poblanos in that the original owners, the Rosengarten family, were very involved with property after Thomas Sears designed the terraces surrounding the residence. The current gardening staff at Chanticleer has enhanced the original tree and shrub planting with wildlife-supporting native plants. The garden uses harvested rainwater to support the planting, and the staff is undertaking many other ecological initiatives to guide the gardens in climate uncertainty.

Dunbarton Oaks, the fifty-three-acre estate of Robert and Mildred Bliss in Georgetown in Washington, DC, is the work of Beatrix Farrand, another of the few female landscape architects who were too accomplished to ignore in the early days of American landscape architecture. Born in 1872, at the beginning of the Country Place era, Farrand developed the Dunbarton Oaks landscape with Mildred Bliss over an eighteen-year period beginning in 1922. Farrand was the only female founding member of the American Society of Landscape Architects in 1899, yet she preferred to call herself a landscape gardener, perhaps because her early experiences combining native plants in garden spaces during childhood summers at Reef Point Estate in Mount Desert Island, Maine, and her internship at the Arnold Arboretum became the basis of her facility with plants as a garden designer.

Charles Sprague Sargent, director of Harvard's Arnold Arboretum from 1872 until 1927, was Farrand's mentor. In the insular world of ornamental horticulture, Sargent, Olmsted, and William Robinson, a British landscape gardener and prolific writer, exchanged plants and correspondence. Farrand was inspired by the work of Robinson and his close friend and colleague Gertrude Jekyll and by Italian Renaissance gardens. Those influences are evident at Dunbarton Oaks in the strong relationship between the architecture and the natural environment. Formal terraced gardens step downslope to garden rooms, some with expansive views. Extensive mixed annual and perennial borders, a rose garden, and a meandering trail to the wild garden along Rock Creek unfolded across the landscape. The smallest of the garden rooms, the Star

Garden with its zodiac motif, was likely known to Ruth Simms and Rose Greely, both Georgetown residents in the 1920s. The zodiac pebble mosaic in the Greely Rose Garden at Los Poblanos may be a nod to Beatrix Farrand. Dunbarton Oaks's sixteen-acre formal gardens passed into the ownership of Harvard University as a research center in 1940, and the twenty-seven-acre wild garden was donated to the National Park Service as Dunbarton Oaks Park, a well-used public green space.

Blithewold, the Van Wickle family's thirty-three-acre estate in Bristol, Rhode Island, also relates to Los Poblanos in a surprising number of ways, despite its Atlantic coast location. Master-planned by John DeWolf with colonial revival and American arts and crafts influences, the gardens were designed with input from an independent mother and her daughters for active use as well as for display. A Lord and Burnham greenhouse at Blithewold predates the one at Los Poblanos by a quarter century, but both are still used by caretakers. The waterfront exposure, although completely different in its impact on plant choices, is just as demanding as the high desert climate of New Mexico.

Country Places in the West

Country places in the West borrowed Renaissance revival and beaux arts formality, symmetry, order, and ornamentation but were also influenced by Spanish and Mediterranean motifs and the arts and crafts movement, which in the landscape meant overflowing shrub and perennial masses à la Gertrude Jekyll and the wild gardens of William Robinson. The awe-inspiring and ore-rich Rocky Mountains and especially our American Mediterranean, the California coast, drew many more Country Place builders than did the more challenging interior deserts.

Hearst Castle in San Simeon, California, where William Randolph Hearst, with the assistance of architect Julia Morgan, developed his famous estate on ranchland above the Pacific coastline, includes eight acres of gardens surrounding the main house of more than one hundred rooms. The estate was developed from 1919 to 1947, was designed for lavish entertaining, and is now managed by California State Parks as a historic property. Cecil Pragnell, an English gardener and landscape architect, who worked in Queen Victoria's botanic gardens in England before emigrating to North America in 1910, was one of the skilled influences employed early on at Hearst Castle. Pragnell's knowledge and experience ran deep, as his father had accompanied Charles Darwin on the HMS *Beagle*, and Pragnell the younger accompanied his father plant hunting in Africa.

Casa del Herrero, the House of the Blacksmith, is an eleven-acre estate in Montecito, California, built in 1925 for George Fox Steedman, a businessman and inventor who was awarded forty patents. Metalwork was his forte, and he created much of the ironwork for his Spanish colonial revival home designed by George Washington Smith. Befitting the architecture and climate, the Moorish-inspired gardens are the work of Ralph Stevens, Lockwood de Forest, and Francis T. Underhill. The house and garden became a national historic landmark in 2009 and are owned and managed by the nonprofit Casa Del Herrero Foundation as a museum, with restoration and preservation goals and objectives similar to the gentle use preservation strategies at Los Poblanos Inn and Organic Farm.

Lotusland near Santa Barbara, California, was initially called Cuesta Linda. The circa-1916 estate of the Gravit family was purchased by Ganna Walska, a Polish opera star and socialite, in 1941. The Gravit gardens included water stairs and a cypress allée,

which were absorbed into the dramatically eccentric personal fantasy that Walska, in collaboration with Lockwood de Forest, an orientalist, artist, and landscape architect, built on the thirty-seven-acre site. More than three thousand plant species organized in themes create a compelling botanic garden that has been open to the public since 1993. There are many other Country Place–era gardens in California, offering a coastal melding of Mediterranean plants with local natives in conditions quite foreign to the arid interior of the Southwest.

Scotty's Castle in Grapevine Canyon, an oasis in Death Valley at the eastern edge of California, is perhaps the oddest collaboration in the story of country places replete with eccentric personalities. Teaming Albert Johnson, an insurance magnate from Chicago, with Walter Scott, a con man so affable that the partnership held well after his scam was uncovered, the Death Valley ranch was developed between 1922 and 1931. Begun as the winter vacation spot of Johnson and his wife, Bessie, it has been described architecturally as Spanish colonial revival. Because of the severity of the climate, construction ceased more often in July and August than in winter. The intense summer heat has kept the landscape mostly native, including oasis palms and desert shrubs as well as cacti and succulents. The National Park Service became the steward of the site, and it has been kept viable through tourism. In 2015 slow-moving storm cells, typical of the changing climate, dumped three inches of rain in Grapevine Canyon and, for the first time in the site's nearly century-long history, caused significant flood damage. It is admirable that the National Park Service has used flood remediation as a learning opportunity, giving tours to show storm water mitigation strategies as it repairs the damage and works to make the site more resilient in future storm events.

Taliesin West in Arizona, Frank Lloyd Wright's winter home and laboratory of architecture, is an anomaly as a country place but enduring as an educational mecca. It began as an experimental campsite at the foot of the McDowell Mountains northeast of Scottsdale and was developed under Wright's immediate influence from 1937 until his death in 1959. Taliesin West became an architectural training center, a place to test new ideas and materials, and is now a UNESCO World Heritage Site. Responsive to the setting embedded in the desert landscape, it is a celebration of local materials: native rock and Sonoran Desert plants. When it was first developed, lawns—the negative space that balances the array of ornamental plants in most landscape design—were a given of that time. Although lawn areas now seem visually discordant and are ecologically unsustainable, they provide green space for visitors and residents and are used adjacent to paving as a softer, cooler alternative to hardscaped gathering spaces. Taliesin West is not typical of the majority of Country Place gardens as there is less transition between exotic and native, no farming or ranching component, less formality and rigidity, and more flow and experimentation in both architecture and landscaping.

The Broadmoor Hotel, designed with the same opulence as a country estate, is included here because of its present-day evolution. The Colorado Springs hotel opened in 1918, conceived as a grand hotel in the European style, offering elegant accommodations, spa amenities, fine dining, and excellent service in the rugged Rocky Mountain foothills. The Italian revival–style architecture and formal bilateral symmetry of the entrance landscape are intentionally anomalous in the rugged setting. Frederick Law Olmsted Jr., the talented son of the renowned father of American landscape architecture, was commissioned to design the three-thousand-acre grounds, and Donald Ross, a golf architect, designed the first golf course. Through grand times, the Depression, wars, and their aftermath, the Broadmoor has survived more than a century and is now an expansive resort that has diversified over the years to include a polo field, riding arena, Olympic training center, ski area, concert venue, and two additional golf courses. Meticulously maintained gardens are the foreground to spectacular native scenery. The scale of Broadmoor is much grander than that of Los Poblanos, but both were conceived from the same gestalt and have persisted by adapting to the times in quite different ways. Climate change poses similar challenges to both, but the scale of Broadmoor and its golf courses will demand greater course correction.

The Country Place era drew to a close in the East and Midwest with the Great Depression, but on the frontier, in New Mexico, it persisted. The arid Southwest has a singularly diverse landscape topographically, climatically, and culturally. The resilient Native people alone represented hundreds of independent groups before Spaniards, Mexicans, and finally Anglo-Americans arrived on the scene. Subsistence farming had been the mainstay of the economy for thousands of years, and given the extremes of heat and cold and the aridity, that was not an easy row to hoe. This sampling of western country places, as varied as they are, shows that they are similar in taking full advantage of their sites adjacent to a perennial water source. Reflecting local culture and evolving to fit current uses, many were working ranches first, palatial mansions second. These were all characteristics shared by Los Poblanos, although it is unique in being architecturally significant. A brief look at a few New Mexican country places offers a glimpse of how they differ from other estates of the era and how they have evolved through time.

Country Places in New Mexico

Castle Huning once reigned over the land along Central Avenue between Old Town and downtown Albuquerque. Although it no longer exists, it is an example of the transition from mid-1800s rural residences (as envisioned by Andrew Jackson Downing) to beaux arts country places, and it touches on Los Poblanos in important ways. Franz Huning, an entrepreneur and community activist, was instrumental in locating a railroad hub in Albuquerque. Huning was also a land speculator; he briefly owned the land that is now Los Poblanos many years before Albert Simms bought it. In 1883 Huning built his empire, inspired by castles along the Rhine River in Germany, on four hundred acres of marshland, sloughs, and pastures. The pastures were used to feed the livestock that hauled his trade goods. He operated a grain mill there and designed and built his grand mansion of *terrones* (sod bricks cut from his land), imitating an Italian villa in a style that was a generation out of fashion by the time it was built. The castle was surrounded by an orchard, vineyard, and vegetable gardens that extended between what is now Fifteenth Street and the Rio Grande. Huning also experimented with exotic tree planting, including catalpa (*C. speciosa*), Osage orange (*Maclura pomifera*), and Lombardy poplars (*Populus nigra*). He lived until 1905, long enough to experience the erratic flooding of the Rio Grande eroding his fields.

After his death, Huning's heirs gradually subdivided the estate, and once the Middle Rio Grande Conservancy District was established to control the flooding, developed it into what is now the Huning Castle Addition, including the Aldo Leopold Historic District and the Albuquerque Country Club neighborhoods. Manzano Day School, an elementary school dedicated to "joy in learning," was founded by Ruth Simms, doyenne of Los Poblanos, in 1938. The school was first housed in the Castle Huning, but when the structure was deemed structurally unsound in 1942, Manzano Day School moved across Central Avenue to La Glorieta, the Huning family's home before Castle Huning was built. Noted Albuquerque authors Erna and Harvey Fergusson, siblings and grandchildren of Franz Huning, grew up at La Glorieta. The Manzano Day School has grown and prospered on the La Glorieta site. Huning Castle Apartments, offering luxury amenities, were built where the original Castle Huning was demolished.

Las Acequias Farm, near Nambe north of Santa Fe, was historically part of a Spanish land grant to Vincente Duran de Armijo in 1739. Cyrus McCormick III, a distant relation of Ruth Simms by her first marriage, purchased ninety-six acres there and in the early 1930s engaged John Gaw Meem to design a Pueblo revival–style home. The farm, located along the Rio Nambe, was sold in 1949 to Robert and Louise McKinney, who were then publishers of the *New Mexican*, the oldest newspaper company in the West. Las Acequias was passed on to Robin McKinney Martin and her husband, Meade Martin, in 1990. There are many parallels to Los Poblanos. The Martins raised their family on the farm, which produced hay, comb honey, eggs, and peacocks. In 2007 Las Acequias was donated as a conservation easement to the New Mexico Land Conservancy to preserve the land in perpetuity for agriculture, as scenic open space, and as wildlife habitat. In 2014 the Meem-designed home was approved for the National Register of Historic Places at the state level. Preservation and a regenerative land ethic are alive and well at Las Acequias, which is still

The Castle Huning landscape, circa 1895, with Castle Huning in the far background. Franz Huning was a successful businessman and gentleman farmer, with the interest and financial wherewithal to build green-houses and plant the vineyard shown here. PA2011.001.055, Albuquerque Museum, gift of James H. Mielke.

operating as a farm and as a commercial producer of compost.

El Rancho de la Mariposa, the Lineberry estate in Taos, was first developed by Duane Van Vechten, a Chicago artist. She first built her studio there in 1929. A few years later, she and her husband, Edwin Lineberry, completed their expansive residence and fourteen acres of gardens, most enclosed in adobe walls and wrought iron fencing. Later, a state-of-the-art 14,415-square-foot museum was added to the studio. In 2018 Taos Pueblo bought back the property, restoring what it called "the gateway to life" to the pueblo.

Relearning the Lessons of Nature

The reclaiming of ancestral land by modern tribal societies is ongoing in New Mexico, and the land ethic shared by Native people could become a great advantage for New Mexico in adapting to climate change. No land is truly wild and undisturbed by human intervention in our time, but the traditional land stew-ardship of the original peoples was based on a deep understanding of place. Native plants can evolve to be better adapted to their growing conditions in as little as three generations. For wildflowers, grasses, and some shrubs, that is a short three years. In the West, we are fortunate to have so many ecological niches for plants to adapt to. Maintaining natural areas in concert with ecological processes allows plants to adapt or migrate to survive and reproduce. Finessed human intervention to curb both exotic plant invasions and catastrophic wildfire disturbance allows natural systems to evolve solutions to climate change. As a species, human beings tend to single-mindedly interfere with natural processes. We need to develop deeper ties with nature, to trust her wisdom, if we are to undo the damage we have already done.

NAN Ranch in Faywood is one of two country places in southern New Mexico that continue as working ranches. It began in 1860 as farm fields along the Mimbres River, raising alfalfa (*Medicago sativa*), corn (*Zea mays*), fruit trees, and cattle. Within a decade, one thousand acres were irrigated, a flour mill was in operation, and more than three thousand head of cattle grazed on nearby rangeland. Close to the Rio Mimbres, the land held evidence of Mogollon settlements dated from 600 to 1140 CE, which merited a visit from early ethnographer, archaeologist, and historian Adolph Bandelier in 1883. In 1927 the land was purchased by John T. McElroy, a wealthy Texas rancher, who commissioned Trost and Trost Engineers and Architects of El Paso to build an expansive Spanish colonial revival house with a

swimming pool and other ranch buildings landscaped with cottonwoods (*Populus* spp.), mulberries (*Morus alba*), Italian cypress (*Cupressus sempervirens*), English ivy (*Hedera helix*), roses (*Rosa* species and cultivars), hollyhocks (*Alcea rosea*), and irises (*Iris germanica*) enclosed by privet (*Ligustrum* spp.) hedges. By 1945 the estate was part of one hundred thousand acres owned by another Texas rancher, W. B. Hinton. NAN Ranch was eighty acres of headquarters surrounded by thousands of acres of desert rangeland cut by seasonally flooded arroyos, spring-fed creeks in shaded canyons, and the Mimbres River. The ranch was added to the National Register of Historic Places in 1988, and ranch income is currently supplemented by vacation rentals.

Coe Ranch in Glencoe is currently a 245-acre cattle operation with 88 acres of senior water rights and six functional wells for irrigation and domestic use. The history of people here includes an association with Billy the Kid, whom the Coe brothers backed in the Lincoln County War. George Coe died in a shootout. Frank Coe wisely left the area briefly but returned to land purchased from Susan McSween and developed his ranch. The original house on the site was built in the late 1800s and had mud and rock walls nearly two feet thick, with gunports at intervals to defend against Mescalero Apaches, who occasionally objected to the taking of their traditional hunting grounds. This structure likely evolved into the relatively modest adobe hacienda, measuring six thousand square feet, which along with an iconic red barn is the heart of the ranch today. Typical of New Mexico country places, a snowmelt-fed stream, in this case the Ruidoso River, runs through the ranch. A beautiful rock-lined acequia irrigates the lawns, cottonwoods (*Populus* spp.), weeping willows (*Salix babylonica*), spruce (*Picea* spp.), roses

Los Luceros, akin to Los Poblanos, offers a glimpse back across time thanks to ongoing preservation efforts. Meandering pathways with interpretive signage make it easy to revisit, imagine, and experience the Country Place era in landscape history, but Los Luceros is frozen in the past while Los Poblanos is resiliently adapting to the present and anticipating the future. Photograph by the author.

(*Rosa* species and cultivars), and perennial beds of the Coe gardens. Apple (*Malus domestica*) and pear (*Pyrus communis*) orchards are also part of the historic landscape, which is surrounded by native piñon (*Pinus edulis*) and alligator juniper (*Juniperus deppeana*) woodland.

Rancho Los Luceros, on the west bank of the Rio Grande near Alcalde, is perhaps the Country Place story that most closely parallels that of Los Poblanos in its origins, with evidence of Puebloan people at least as early as 1400 BCE. Spanish history here has been documented since the early 1700s, when a grant of fifty thousand acres for service to the crown was awarded to Sebastian and

Antonio Martin-Serrano. They built a four-room farmhouse that grew into a twenty-four-room hacienda, which was occupied by Martin-Serrano descendants until 1882. A series of reverses reduced the estate to the present-day 180 acres purchased for back taxes in 1923 by Mary Cabot Wheelwright, Boston heiress, cultural preservationist, and benefactor of New Mexico arts. Her tenure marks the Country Place evolution, as Wheelwright extensively restored the ranch and lived there seasonally until her death in 1958. The garden included a heritage apple orchard, and churro sheep grazed the acequia-flooded pastures.

Rancho Los Luceros was willed to the Wheelwright Foundation and then, passing through many interim owners, suffered a sad decline. In 1982 Malcolm Grimmer nominated the two-story territorial-style hacienda, the chapel, and two other buildings to the National Register of Historic Places. Acknowledging the cultural significance of the site did not keep it from further deterioration and foreclosure a few years later. The ranch was sold to the American Studies Foundation and then purchased and fully restored by Frank and Ann Cabot, Wheelwright's granddaughter. It was ultimately purchased by the New Mexico Department of Cultural Affairs as a cultural destination, and while age and wear have taken a toll on the interior of the main house, the chapel and some smaller residences have been refurbished. The site itself remains 148 well-tended acres.

Batten House in Albuquerque's North Valley is also a well-preserved country place, now under the aegis of the Albuquerque Museum Foundation and open to the public only for specific small events. Originally the Juan Cristobal Armijo "New Homestead," it is located at the eastern edge of the old village of Los Griegos, which was incorporated into the city of Albuquerque in the 1950s. While most of the early haciendas in the North Valley were destroyed in floods that both plagued the valley and benefited farming there, the Armijo property likely survived because it sat at the edge of a low hill that protected it from the Rio's erratic behavior. The old farmhouse that became the west wing of the hacienda at Los Poblanos was likely the old Armijo homestead. The New Homestead was built circa 1875 in traditional style, as a series of rooms opening onto a central placita, or courtyard, with a classic zaguan entryway—with double doors wide enough to allow carriage entrance and a smaller pedestrian main door. The New Homestead property remained in the hands of the extended Armijo family until 1930, when it was purchased by the Borrell family, who restored and preserved the hacienda and built a large pond, renaming their country place Hacienda del Lago. Baroness Lucia von Borosini, at the time the wife of Edmund Engel, Albuquerque city manager, bought the property in 1952 and called it Outlook Ranch.

With her last husband, Harry Batten, a Philadelphia advertising tycoon, she restored the gardens and built a library west of the original hacienda to house her eclectic book collection. The gardens still include a run-wild jujube grove (*Ziziphus jujuba*), but the pecan (*Carya illinoinensis*) orchard along the acequia, white-fruiting Nanking cherries (*Prunus tomentosa* var. *Leucocarpa*), katsura trees (*Cercidiphyllum japonicum*), and Chinese flame tree (*Koelreuteria bipinnata*) or Taiwan flame gold (*Koelreuteria elegans* spp. *formosana*) that created a woodland east of the hacienda are suffering from the current severe drought. The white Nanking cherry, with larger, sweeter fruit than the species, and the raintree species with rose-colored papery seedpods rarely seen in New Mexico, may be the result of Lucia Batten's wide-ranging travels, from which she returned home with art, textiles, and other artifacts, including experimental plants to try in her gardens. She lived at Outlook Ranch until her death in 2005. She bequeathed the property that has come to be known as Batten House, and all its contents, to the Albuquerque Museum Foundation to occupy and maintain in perpetuity. Batten House figures in the gardens of Los Poblanos much more directly than the other country places in having been the inspiration for the lotus pond and the source of some of the peafowl that have become permanent residents at Los Poblanos.

Sources, and an Invitation to Dig Deeper

Biltmore. "Gardens & Grounds." Biltmore, 2022, https://www.biltmore.com/visit/biltmore-estate/gardens-grounds.

Blithewold, "Blithewold's Gardens: The Arts and Crafts Movement in Full Bloom." Blithewold, 2022, https://www.blithewold.org/about/gardens.

Broadmoor. "Broadmoor Historical Timeline." Broadmoor, 2022, https://www.broadmoor.com/the-resort/historical-timeline.

Chanticleer, https://www.chanticleergarden.org.

Cultural Landscape Foundation. "Ellen Shipman." Cultural Landscape Foundation, 2022, https://www.tclf.org/pioneer/ellen-shipman.

Davis, Brain, and Thomas Oles. "From Architecture to Landscape." *Places*, October 2014, https://doi.org/10.22269/141013.

Death Valley National Park. "Building Scotty's Castle." Death Valley National Park, https://www.nps.gov/deva/learn/historyculture/building-scottys-castle.htm, accessed October 27, 2022.

Downing, Andrew Jackson. *A Treatise on the Theory and Practice of Landscape Gardening Adapted to North America*. New York: Wiley and Putnam, 1844.

Dumbarton Oaks. "About the Garden Archives." Dumbarton Oaks, 2022, https://www.doaks.org/library-archives/garden-archives.

Frank Lloyd Wright Foundation. "Taliesin West Is Frank Lloyd Wright's Desert Laboratory in Arizona." Frank Lloyd Wright Foundation, https://franklloydwright.org/talies-in-west.

Gardenvisit. "History & Theory: Landscape Architecture." Gardenvisit, 2002, https://www.gardenvisit.com/history_theory/library_online_ebooks/ml_gothein_history_garden_art_design/pliny_youngers_villas_garden_letters.

Graham, Wade. *American Eden from Monticello to Central Park to Our Backyards: What Our Gardens Tell Us About Ourselves*. New York: Harper Collins, 2011.

Guzmán, Alicia Inez. "If These Walls Could Talk." *New Mexico Magazine*, March 12, 2019, https://www.newmexico.org/nmmagazine/articles/post/los-luceros-historic-hacienda.

Historic Hotels of America. "The Broadmoor." Historic Hotels of America, 2022, https://www.historichotels.org/us/hotels-resorts/the-broadmoor/history.php.

Kammer, David. "Aldo Leopold Neighborhood Historic District." Living Places, 2022, https://www.livingplaces.com/NM/Bernalillo_County/Albuquerque_City/Aldo_Leopold_Neighborhood_Historic_District.html.

Major, Judith K. *To Live in the New World: A. J. Downing and American Landscape Gardening*. Cambridge, MA: MIT Press, 1997.

Mozingo, Louise A., and Linda L. Jewell, eds. *Women in Landscape Architecture: Essays on History and Practice*. Jefferson, NC: McFarland, 2012.

Nolan, Frederick. *The West of Billy the Kid*. Norman: University of Oklahoma Press, 1998.

Robinson, William, and Rick Darke. *The Wild Garden*. Portland, OR: Timber Press, 2010.

Waring, Gwendolyn L. *A Natural History of the Intermountain West, Its Ecological and Evolutionary Story*. Salt Lake City: University of Utah Press, 2011.

Weiser, Kathy, ed. "Scotty's Castle in Death Valley

National Park." Legends of America, 2022,
https://www.legendsofamerica.com/ca-
scottyscastle.

Wilson, William H. *The City Beautiful Movement*. Baltimore: Johns Hopkins University
Press, 1989.

CHAPTER 3

The Development of the Simms Country Place at Los Poblanos, 1932-1964

Gardens are the slowest of the performing arts, and their lives can long exceed ours.
—Mac Griswold, garden historian

Unlike some other country places, whose ownership stories are tumultuous, Los Poblanos has had the great advantage of a continuum of only a few personally vested owners over nearly a century. Many country places, especially those in the East, were second residences and summer homes. Los Poblanos differed in being the primary home of the Simms and Rembe families and was a working farm most of that time. Agricultural land in the Los Poblanos area had captured the interest of speculators, and during the Country Place era, ownership was sometimes brief but profitable. Franz Huning, a key player in the development of Albuquerque, acquired the property from the Garcia, Torres, Lucero, and Zamora families and quickly sold the combined acreage to Charles Etheridge. In 1899 Jacob Peter Jacobson, a Danish immigrant, arrived in New Mexico to work for the Santa Fe Railway, and by 1902 he had purchased the property with his wife, a woman with

legendary butter-making skills. With a few Jersey cows, the Jacobsons started a dairy farm that years later would become part of the Simmses' Los Poblanos Ranch. By the 1920s dairies had become a large part of the agricultural economy in the Albuquerque area, and the Jacobsons joined a dozen or so neighboring dairy owners in the Albuquerque Cooperative Dairy Association, a practical means of collecting, processing, and marketing milk for multiple small family farms.

Albert Gallatin Simms was a relative newcomer to New Mexico, having come west with his young wife, Katherine, to recover from tuberculosis in 1920. She was the wealthy great-granddaughter of early Harvard University president Increase Mather. Simms recovered, but his wife died the following year. He honored her memory by endowing the Katherine Mather Simms Award for English Composition at the University of New Mexico, still awarded to a female upperclassman annually.

Simms, a lawyer, banker, and great reader, was said to be largely self-taught. He proved to be an astute businessman, recognizing opportunities as they arose, and quickly gained local prominence, first in business and then in politics.

Albert Simms is known primarily through reports of his activities: land purchases, livestock breeding successes, business and political offices, and board positions. He greatly respected and admired his brother John, who moved with him to New Mexico for tuberculosis treatment in Silver City in 1912, the same year New Mexico became a state. Albert Simms studied law and was admitted to the bar in 1915, but by 1920 he had developed an interest in banking. He served jointly on the Albuquerque City Council and the Bernalillo County Commission—for two years as the commission's chair. Simms bought 110 acres, including the present-day site of Los Poblanos, from Wylie Williams in 1928. John Field Simms purchased the adjacent property to the south in 1931. Los Poblanos began a long-term transition from Hispanic to Anglo ownership, reuniting and maintaining the large land grant tracts for farming and ranching. After serving a two-year term in the New Mexico House of Representatives, Albert Simms was elected to the seventy-first US Congress, where he met Ruth Hanna McCormick.

Hanna had grown up in a politically prominent family and in the early twentieth century often sat next to President Theodore Roosevelt at the family dinner table. Nurtured in a political milieu, she eventually married her soulmate, Medill McCormick, scion of the *Chicago Tribune* McCormick family and future senator from Illinois. In *Ruth Hanna McCormick, a Life in Politics 1800–1944,* Kristie Miller notes McCormick making an important distinction between her political and personal outlooks: "I am a suffragist, not a femi-

nist," she said. This impeccably dressed mother of three, former personal assistant to her powerful father, Senator Marcus Hanna, and political asset to her husband, challenged the limited role women of her generation were expected to play. She had higher aspirations and the skills to realize them, and she advanced politically with the support of newly voting women. Her goal was to fully integrate women into the partisan political process, but not as a women's bloc. After Medill McCormick's death, Ruth ran for an at-large congressional seat from Illinois and credited the support of black women, a doubly disenfranchised group, for her win.

Albert Simms met Ruth McCormick while serving in Congress from 1929 to 1931. Both Republicans had recently lost their beloved spouses, and they struck up a sympathetic friendship. The political climate in Washington took a decided turn in 1930. The Depression, Prohibition, and President Hoover's unpopularity had shifted the country toward Democrats, and neither Simms nor McCormick won reelection. Having grown up in a political household, McCormick was apparently resigned to the shifting tide on the national scene.

After a rather low-key courtship, Simms and McCormick married in 1932 and came to New Mexico to live. This was the beginning of the Country Place–era gardens of Los Poblanos and a revival of farming as an experimental enterprise on the land.

Gregarious, charming, and full of life, Ruth Simms, early suffragist, newspaper publisher, activist, politician, accomplished horsewoman, and rancher in Illinois and Colorado, may have been both perfectly suited to taking up a new life in frontier New Mexico and a surprising challenge as a wife to the more conservative, more reserved Albert Simms. Both were interested in raising cat-

Beautiful and well built, the 1934 dairy barn was used to house the Simms herd and occasionally as a gathering space for ranch fiestas. Its use now changes with need; it provides space for drying lavender, storage, and other service-related activities. Photograph by the author.

tle and had the financial means to join the burgeoning local dairy industry. Albert bred Guernsey cattle. And Ruth brought a herd of prize-winning Holstein-Friesians with her to New Mexico. During the 1930s and 1940s the Simmses acquired thirty parcels of land near Los Poblanos, much of it from the heirs to the Elena Gallegos Land Grant. In 1938 they acquired the eastern portion of the original grant, seventeen thousand acres of grazing land extending from the foothills to the crest of the Sandia Mountains. The land had been used for communal grazing and was heavily degraded

by drought and overuse. It became Los Poblanos Ranch grazing land, hardly profitable as such but an astute investment as reflected by future land values.

Ruth Simms sought out John Gaw Meem to design the addition to the existing farmhouse as the Simms residence. Soon afterward, Simms and Meem embarked on the La Quinta project, a quietly impressive cultural center. Meem was at the time the preeminent New Mexico architect, famous for creating up-to-date facilities expressed in a traditional regional style true to their place. An

engineer by training, Meem respected the suitability of Pueblo architecture to the hot, dry climate of the Southwest. He used local materials and refined traditional methods in a straightforward, logical way to create comfortable living spaces for his clients. The territorial revival–style residence and adjacent La Quinta epitomize New Mexico architecture. With the complementary gardens designed by landscape architect Rose Greely, Los Poblanos Ranch was elevated as a unique and premier example of a country place.

To transform the farmhouse, which is believed to be the old Armijo homestead, into the Simms hacienda, wings were added to the original 1800s adobe, enclosing a central courtyard with a zaguan, a traditional carriage entrance. Los Poblanos's zaguan connected the east portal and the central courtyard placita, a gracious link between two outdoor living spaces well suited to buffering the desert climate in all seasons. La Quinta, designed as

an entertainment center, was ideally situated to be both accessible to the residence and separate from it. The north wing of La Quinta housed the library and gallery. The west wing was the ballroom, and the south wing included guest rooms. The east side was open to mountain views. Drawing upon characteristics of Renaissance villas, wide *portales*, the traditional covered porches of adobe architecture, wrapped all three sides of the east courtyard with a sweeping farm-to-desert to mountain view. A gazebo-roofed terrace on the west side of the ballroom opened onto another more intimate garden space.

The Design of the Gardens of Los Poblanos

Ruth Simms enlisted the skills of Rose Greely, one of the first female licensed architects and landscape architects in the United States. Los Poblanos was

The zaguan doorway into the placita was one of John Gaw Meem's references to historic architectural features. Both Meem and Simms valued function; the zaguan is not a hollow homage to the past but continues to be a useful feature. Photograph by the author.

Greely's only project in the West, and here she freely combined beaux arts formality and arts and crafts regionalism, setting a precedent for xeriscape, a landscape design style that developed fifty years later in response to western water constraints. Both Greely in the 1930s and xeriscape in the 1980s placed the highest water use near the buildings, in the most highly used spaces. Per arts and crafts movement precepts, the landscape was relaxed in style and had native plants in perimeter areas, transitioning from highly designed to more natural farther from buildings. Greely's modus operandi was creating harmony between different styles and the architecture, including artisan craft details such

as pebble mosaic pavement, and Moorish-inspired water features. In an overall parklike setting, she created several outdoor living rooms.

In contrast to the lush, treed landscape of present-day Los Poblanos, the early gardens were sunbaked and exposed, with an east view of the Sandia Mountains and a view of the basalt volcanic cones on the mesa to the west rising beyond the bosque—the cottonwood (*Populus deltoides* spp. *wislizeni*) and willow (*Salix* spp.) woodland along the Rio Grande. All the garden plans she drew included several tree-planting options for shade and wind protection. Several existing sheets of plans for the west garden and the placita include multiple options, labeled "schemes," for planting combinations based on color, form, and seasonality. There was both separation and easy transition between the Simms residence and La Quinta, the guest house and cultural center. North of the residence was a sunken, acequia-irrigated cutting garden and greenhouse used for breeding roses and chrysanthemums. The allée of Siberian elms (*Ulmus pumila*) and cottonwoods continues to be an elegant approach to Los Poblanos. Rose Greely was also interested in experimental agriculture, so she may have been consulted in plotting areas for the early Los Poblanos cultivation of sugar beets (*Beta vulgaris*), alfalfa (*Medicago sativa*), oats (*Avena sativa*), barley (*Hordeum vulgare*), and corn (*Zea mays*), but there is no confirmation of that in the archives.

Books in La Quinta's large library were available to be checked out by people in the Los Ranchos community. The art gallery hosted varied cultural events, including readings by Thornton Wilder, Witter Bynner, and Paul Horgan. The library, gallery, and ballroom, able to accommodate concerts for 120 guests, were directly linked to the east-facing courtyard with the panorama of the Sandia Mountains viewed across Albuquerque's first swimming pool. Doors carved by Gustave Baumann opened onto the Grand Portal—generously proportioned covered porches embellished with a Peter Hurd fresco of San Ysidro, patron of farmers; Robert Woodman tinwork; and ironwork fixtures by Walter Gilbert, including plowshare-inspired door handles and the elegant wrought iron garden gates. Local artists and craftspeople were celebrated at a time when commissions were much needed in hard economic times. This was the Simmses' private market–driven answer to the Works Progress Administration (WPA).

Whether muted by the vastness of the desert setting or the quiet aptness of the more expansive La Quinta, the Country Place landscape design was more subdued at Los Poblanos, more reflective of its place in the Rio Grande Valley of New Mexico than evocative of Old World opulence. The agricultural emphasis was perhaps more pronounced, fitting in a frontier town poised on the edge of urbanity. The surrounding landscape was a mosaic of farm fields crosscut by acequias, the irrigation canals that made farming there possible. The blend of beaux arts formality and arts and crafts earthiness that Rose Greely wove in concert with Ruth Simms was certainly the most sophisticated landscape design in Albuquerque at the time, a complement to the cultural amenities offered in the architecture the gardens surrounded.

The Ruth Simms and Rose Greely Collaboration

How did these two women, so ahead of their time in so many ways, come to develop an enduring garden in conditions so foreign to both their past experiences? In her relatively short tenure in New Mexico, Ruth Simms—transplanted from Illinois via Washington, DC, to this extensive property between the Rio Grande and the foothills of the Sandia Mountains—was to have an indelible impact on her community and the evolution of gardens there.

Ruth Simms's daughter Katrina McCormick Barnes noted that her mother had worked with Rose Greely on her garden in Georgetown while Ruth was serving in Congress, so there was a link already established. Greely was well traveled and well schooled. The opportunity to design six acres of gardens at Los Poblanos was well within her scope of work. She was an early graduate of an architecture and landscape architecture program

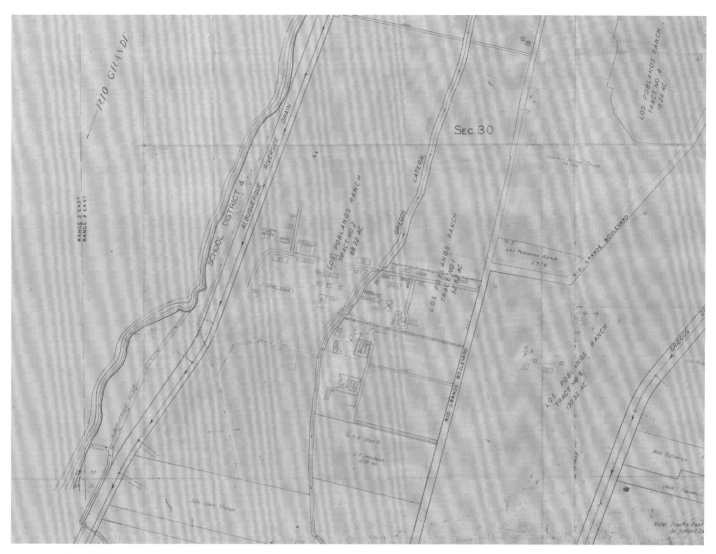

This 1937 map shows the part of Los Poblanos Ranch irrigated by the Griegos Lateral. The map includes the footprint of the hacienda and La Quinta. Note the spread of the Rio Grande compared with the channel today. Map 030, courtesy of the Middle Rio Grande Conservancy District.

for women collaborated upon by the Cambridge School of Design, Harvard, and MIT, and cooperative farming had been the subject of her thesis in 1920, so Simms and Greely also shared an interest in agricultural innovation.

New Mexico has always been a place with web-like ties in the community, two degrees of separation rather than the apocryphal six. As an example of this fine mesh that seems to connect everyone in New Mexico, Faith Bemis was a 1931 graduate of the

Cambridge School of Design program, a decade after Rose Greely. Bemis's aunt Alice Bemis Taylor was a patron of John Gaw Meem in Colorado Springs, and when he was awarded the contract for the Colorado Springs Fine Arts Center, Taylor asked Meem to hire her newly graduated niece as a draftsperson. Within a few years, Faith and John were married, forming a partnership that lasted the rest of their long and accomplished lives. Ruth Simms was already familiar with Meem's work from her tenure on the board of trustees of the Fountain Valley School, another of his projects in Colorado Springs. On the frontier that New Mexico was at the time, having two of the first women trained as architects at the Cambridge School of Design with links to Los Poblanos is remarkable.

Because Greely was a prolific writer, there is ample documentation of her philosophy and professional growth throughout her multi-decade career. In 1932, about when she began work at Los Poblanos, she wrote a series of articles for *House Beautiful* magazine that outlined her design thinking. In the first essay, "Some of the Factors, Both Practical and Aesthetic, That Influence the Design of the Grounds," she argues for the value of design rather than the random showcasing of specimens and horticultural oddities: "The last one hundred years have generated too much interest in horticultural specimens and too little interest in the larger question of design." Greely understood that design is not about showcasing specimens; it is about combining materials to work well in specific places for specific purposes. Her academic training, absorption of the beaux arts design standards of the time, and exposure to the latest design ideas in decorative arts, artisan craftwork, and landscape gave her the credentials to tackle projects from grand estates to cottage surrounds. Greely's competency in architecture led her to weave a bond between buildings and the landscape that serves both well. This focus on design included fluency in planting options as well as strong hardscape features—paving, walls, arbors, and water features—possibly because her interest was in providing experiences in outdoor spaces much deeper than mere decoration. Spaces were to be functional and coherent, an expectation that Greely and Simms appear to have shared.

In the last *House Beautiful* article, titled "Balance and Rhythm in Landscape Design," Greely wrote, "Unless the garden is severely formal, it is entirely permissible and often more interesting to introduce elements of change—a difference of pattern or of color which breaks the symmetry of the design without interrupting its balance." The protected central courtyard, the placita, in the Simms hacienda is an example of a beaux arts garden room. It is formally symmetrical. Its central water feature is a colorfully tiled Moorish star. The potted plants are sheared into geometric shapes. The garden west of the hacienda, while still carefully balanced, is slightly asymmetrical. Here Greely combined the strong lines of paved paths with two water features, connected by a rill flowing down the center of the cross-axial pathway. The planting beds are off center in the space as a whole. Secondary paths divide the garden beds into smaller geometric shapes, which allow more intimate access to the plantings and frame views of the garden from various vantage points. In a harsh and erratic climate, asymmetrical balance is much easier to establish and maintain than bilateral symmetry, so her personal preference aligned with the vagaries of the Southwest climate. When you know the rules, you can bend them effectively.

The gardens of Los Poblanos that Greely designed were the placita courtyard and formal west garden—now aptly called the Rose Greely Garden—the spaces between the residence and La Quinta, the gardens surrounding La Quinta, and the kitchen garden, cutting garden, and greenhouse. Designed landscapes, by their very nature, change over time, even if only because the plants grow and alter the space. Often the built elements are more long-lived than the planting, but trees transcend the boundary between architecture and horticulture, as these long-lived plants can be structural in their presence and persistence. Meem consulted with Simms on the alignment of the approach lane, and it is likely that Greely collaborated on the planting of the iconic allée shaded by Siberian elm (*Ulmus pumila*) and native cottonwood (*Populus deltoides* spp. *wislizeni*). In the desert Southwest, trees are especially valuable for their cooling shade and layers of habitat, and since the natural environment supports relatively few large trees, their selection and placement are crucial to long-term success. At Los Poblanos, partly because of decades of acequia irrigation, the entryway allée, the shade trees in the lawns, and the border plantings have thrived and continue to grace the landscape today.

The Placita Garden

With meticulous attention to detail, John Gaw Meem extended the historic remnant of the existing farmhouse into a gracious traditional residence of four joined wings, a hollow square with central placita, and an inner courtyard that is open to the clear desert sky. The placita was framed by portales—southwestern porches—on all sides and wood-paneled zaguan doors, evoking a wide carriage gate entrance inset with a smaller pedestrian door. Well past horse and carriage days, the zaguan at Los Poblanos is a reference to historic architectural features but in the here and now creates a generous and flexible passage between the interior portal and the east exterior portal that shelters the formal entryway.

The placita garden designed by Greely is the heart of the home, a living space that all the rooms open onto. The north portal is in deep shade in summer, when the sun is north of midsky, and is warmed by the low-angled sun in winter. The north portal includes a corner fireplace for extending use of the space comfortably into

cooler weather. The centerpiece of the placita is a tiled eight-pointed Moorish fountain. The original tiles included some brought home by the Simms from their travels to Spain. While the placita paving is brick and tiles, the portales and exterior paving is pink San Cristobal flagstone; the paving materials suggest the separation of spaces without the barrier of walls. Separated planting beds on the east and west sides of the placita direct circulation on-axis west from the zaguan to the library door with sidelights. There were alternative schemes drawn for the layout of the bricks and tiles around the fountain and several options for plants to fill the spaces.

Planting plans preserved in the Greely archives at the University of Virginia and in the library at La Quinta detail schemes for seasonal color, including spring bulbs such as tulips (*Tulipa*), daffodils (*Narcissus*), hyacinth (*Hyacinthus*), and mariposa lily (*Calochortus*), a western native. Potted plant suggestions included Asian bleeding hearts (*Lamprocapnos*, formerly *Dicentra speciosa*), followed in bloom by pink geraniums (*Pelargoniums*) and blue bellflower (*Campanula*) or alternately by *Freesias*, pansies (*Viola* hybrids), *Petunia* hybrids, and marigolds (*Tagetes*). The potted plants expanded the seasons, as plants that prefer cooler temperatures could be shifted to shaded spaces as needed in summer, replaced by sun lovers that could bask as long as the seasons allowed. The pots also alleviated the rigid symmetry of the hardscape design and evoked a sense of the old Andalusian courtyard gardens of Seville, Granada, and Córdoba.

Vine options included *Wisteria sinensis*, pale pink *Clematis montana* or vivid purple Jackman clematis, and fragrant climbing roses (*Rosa* cultivars), including 'Mary Wallace,' 'Dr. Van Fleet,' and 'Star of Persia.' In this rather confined space, large shrubs, including alternative options of crape

The placita (patio) garden designed by Greely is the heart of the home. All the rooms straddling the divide between house and garden open onto this space. While the plants that enliven the space have changed over the past ninety years, the sense of serenity persists. File 105, Albert and Shirley Small Special Collections Library, University of Virginia.

myrtle (*Lagerstroemia*) or fringe tree (*Chionanthus virginicus*), filled the role of trees. Mountain ash (*Sorbus americana*), rose acacia (*Robinia hispida*), and golden raintree (*Koelreuteria paniculata*) were also named as canopy options, with *Hypericum repens* as an evergreen groundcover. Planned evergreen shrubs included *Cotoneaster franchettii* trained as standards, strong central stems staked to rigid supports with the terminal branches trimmed to form dense cascading canopies, Italian cypress (*Cupressus sempervirens*) or dwarf yews (*Taxus cuspidata nana*), all very controlled in form and balanced in mass.

The West Garden

Directly opposite the zaguan entrance, the west door in the placita leads through a sitting room to the west terrace, a patio, and a formal garden that has been described as both Italianate and English Renaissance in style. Italianate references include the use of water, symmetry, and formal hedging, while English Renaissance borrowed from Italianate style, with perhaps a stronger connection to the home. Both imply dominance over nature. The west garden has a strong north–south axis

This detail from the site plan of the entire property shows the hacienda placita and the Greely Garden. The garden is still very much as Rose Greely designed it in 1932. Graphic by Hannah Aulick and the author.

cool one's feet in a time before air-conditioning. Siberian irises (*Iris siberica*) surround the sitting walls. The vertical evergreen leaves provide textural interest when not in bloom.

The rill flows down the middle of the east–west axis path, under the farthest north–south pathway, which arches over the east basin and daylights at the edge of the lawn of the hacienda. Pathways neatly divide parterre beds, with wider beds on the east. These axial beds were formally laid out and remain strong architectural elements of the garden. Clay roof tiles border the beds and act as funnels for acequia water to flood the beds. To soften the formality of the design at the south end of the main axis, Simms commissioned New Mexican folk artist "Pop" Shaffer to create pebble mosaics and patterns in the paving, including a circular zodiac motif and Native American symbols. On the terrace immediately west of the residence, Judge, Ruth Simms's prize bull, and Grumpy, Los Poblanos's prize milk producer, are immortalized in mosaics of pebbles and cement.

Greely sketched out several planting schemes for this garden, and it is difficult to discern which was planted initially. As she was very involved in the planning, perhaps Simms chose plants she particularly liked from each of the schemes and combined them. Given the wrinkles in any garden project, availability of the desired plant specimens was certainly as much an issue in the Simms–Greely era as it is currently, so having alternative schemes to choose from must have helped expedite the planting, especially with Greely consulting from a distance and communicating by telegram. It is likely that some of the herbaceous ornamental plants were grown in the greenhouse on site along with bedding vegetables.

As part of the team working on plant selection for both phases of the evolution of Los Poblanos

crosscut by smaller pathways dividing the planting beds. The north–south axis intersects with a wide path divided by a Mudejar water rill linking sunken water basins on the west and far eastern sides of the garden. The Mudejar rill, a landscape feature borrowed from Islamic traditions, was widely used in Spain in the twelfth to the fifteenth centuries to move a trickle of water through a garden. The west basin is screened from the Griegos Lateral, the main acequia that feeds Los Poblanos, and from the blazing afternoon sun with western cane (*Arundo donax*), golden raintree (*Koelreuteria paniculata*), burkwood viburnums (*V. × burkwoodii*, a new hybrid at the time), and green ash (*Fraxinus pennsylvanica*). The east basin has sitting walls on each side, an invitation to rest in the shade and

The *Greely Garden* with Pop Shaffer's pebble mosaic, 2021. Patterns in the paving include a circular zodiac motif (seen at the bottom of the image) and Native American symbols. Parterre beds are neatly defined by pathways, with wider beds on the east. Clay roof tiles border the beds and act as funnels for acequia water. The wisteria arbor shading the inn's Greely Rooms is seen at the far end of the garden. Photograph by the author.

Detail of the Pop Shaffer pebble mosaic, showing a section of the zodiac symbols. Photograph by the author.

Judge and Grumpy, Ruth Simms's prized livestock, are immortalized in the paving. Photograph by the author.

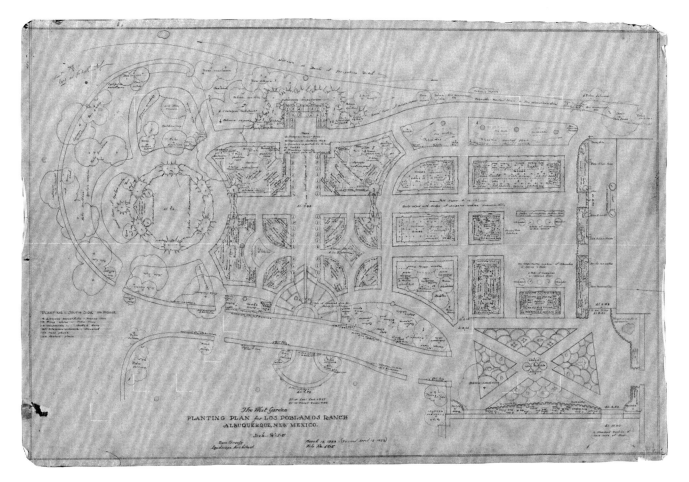

The west garden planting plan, 1933. The west garden is aptly called the Rose Greely Garden to acknowl-edge the enduring work of the landscape architect who created it. It is one of the oldest and best-preserved spaces in the gardens of Los Poblanos. Many of the trees, viburnums, peonies, and Lady Banks roses are original. File 105, Albert and Shirley Small Special Collections Library, University of Virginia.

in 2008 and 2015, I found the copies of archived telegrams between Ruth Simms and Rose Greely concerning materials obtained and options available to be a revelation. (The notion of Simms and Greely communicating by telegram on the initial planning and planting greatly deepened my appreciation of internet technology, especially considering all the emails sent and conference calls made during our second expansion process.) Given the constraints of sourcing materials and establishing the elegant bones of the design, the axial pathways, water basins, and connecting Mudejar rill remain as a frame. Many original plantings blossomed

here and continue to do so. Other plantings were replaced as the decades passed.

The contemporary planting scheme includes apothecary roses—modern-day hybrids of fragrant heritage varieties distilled for their oil and hydrosol. The roses are interplanted with seasonal perennials: spring-blooming daffodils (*Narcissus*), wood violets (*Viola sororia*), and long-lived peonies *Paeonia* that have held their place over the years. Many more peonies have been added in several areas because this deeply rooting perennial evades the heat by blooming early and splendidly, so it is one of the exotics that has found a niche at Los

Daylilies in the Greely Garden. Tawny daylilies, the orange-blooming stalwarts of eastern and midwestern gardens, have proven to be especially well adapted to flood irrigation and continue to star in summer garden beds. Photograph by Wes Brittenham.

Daylilies cut for the kitchen, to grace the plate. Both daylily buds, the "golden needles" of Asian recipes, and the newly open flowers shown here are delicious. Photograph by Wes Brittenham.

Poblanos. Daylilies (*Hemerocallus*), *Phlox paniculata*, and yarrow (*Achillea*) add color in the heat of summer, when the roses take a siesta. Species daylilies, the orange-blooming stalwart of eastern and midwestern gardens, have proven to be especially well adapted to flood irrigation, and they continue to be stars in the summer both in garden beds and gracing the plate in kitchens. Both daylily buds—the "golden needles" of Asian recipes—and newly opened flowers are delicious.

Fried Daylily Flowers Tempura

INGREDIENTS

1 dozen large daylily flowers
with stamens removed
1 cup all-purpose flour
½ cup cornstarch
2 eggs
1 ¼ cups cold sparkling water
8 cups canola oil

Plant Selection Across Time

1. In a 10-inch cast-iron pan, heat the canola oil to 325 degrees and hold at that temperature. Combine the dry ingredients in a medium-size mixing bowl, combine the eggs and cold sparkling water, and then combine the wet and dry mixtures. It is okay if the batter is a bit lumpy. It is also okay to add more water if needed to get the right consistency for a light, crispy flower.

2. Dip the batter-covered blossoms in hot olive oil until lightly browned. When done frying, place on a paper-lined tray and season with salt.

Recipe courtesy of Campo

At some point, a tulip magnolia (*M. × soulangeana*) gained a place of early spring prominence. The wisteria arbor that shades the south portal of the adjacent guest rooms is part of the original planting, as is the enormous salt cedar (*Tamarix* spp.) that sentincls thc north gate of the Greely Garden. The golden raintree (*Koelreuteria paniculata*), burkwood viburnum (*V. × burkwoodii*), lilacs (*Syringa*), piñon pine (*Pinus edulis*), spruce (*Picea* spp.), and crabapples (*Malus domestica* cultivars) that surround the garden on the south and west sides shelter a trio of Japanese maples (*Acer palmatum*). Whether they were all planted at the same time or the maples were planted after the shade canopy and wind buffer were well-established, the tender-leafed Japanese introduction has benefited greatly from growing in the shelter of the robust humidifying backdrop.

This short list of species holds several stories of the evolution of garden plant choices here. The banksia rose (*Rosa banksiae* 'Alba Plena'), viburnum (*V. × burkwoodii*), and wisteria (*W. sinensis*) are all still commonly cultivated in the middle Rio Grande Valley. *Magnolia × soulangeana* and maple (*Acer palmatum*) have always been limited in their use to well-irrigated, wind-sheltered places, a constraint even more impactful today. The golden raintree (*Koelreuteria paniculata*), because of the companion raintree beetle—a small red-and-black insect that does no damage except to reproduce with impunity—currently receives a mixed reception. This is unfortunate because the golden raintree is a beautiful and resilient small tree, giving needed shade in difficult situations. It is one of the plants included in the new gardens for its great adaptability and because of the soft quality of light that filters through the canopy.

Wisteria is another of the original plants included in the contemporary plant palette, but now the native Kentucky wisteria (*W. macrostachya*), as well as *Wisteria sinensis*, is locally available. It tends to remain smaller than the Chinese species, and since it blooms a bit later in spring, it avoids the deep cold snaps that sometimes freeze buds and delay or eliminate the flower show of the Asian wisterias. The floral racemes are not as pendulous in the US native, but it often blooms twice as long. Regardless of origin, wisterias root deeply and are drought-resilient once they are well established.

Many people feel that you cannot have a garden without roses, and there are so many species and varieties that finding the perfect ones for various garden spaces is an embarrassment of riches, an adventure in color, scent, size, and seasonality.

The low humidity and relatively mild winters in Albuquerque are certainly assets in broadening the range of roses that will grow here. Apothecary roses are exceptionally fragrant old varieties of the species including *Rosa gallica officinalis* and hybrids from southern Europe and Turkey to the Caucasus; Damask rose or rose of Castille (*Rosa × damascena*), which is a triple hybrid of *Rosa gallica* and *Rosa fedtschenkoana* with musk rose (*Rosa moschata*); cabbage rose (*Rosa centifolia*), from France and North Africa; and the bourbon rose (*Rosa gallica × Rosa chinensis*), a chance hybrid and "new" introduction in 1820. Aside from their intoxicating fragrances and flower colors, what these old roses share is vigor, disease resistance, and tolerance of light shade and relatively poor soils. In other words, they are excellent roses for a variety of garden niches in the middle Rio Grande Valley.

On the other hand, rose acacia (*Robinia hispida*), a native shrub in the southeastern United States, is not widely cultivated and with some justification is now considered a noxious weed in places to which it was introduced. The benefits of this nitrogen-fixing legume are its ability to tolerate extremes of periodic flooding, drought, and alkaline soils, and its bristliness as a barrier planting. The downsides of rose acacia are its tendency to root sprout aggressively, wherever enough water is available; its fast growth and weak-wooded fragility in windstorms; and its overall tenacity when invading spaces where it is not wanted. I have lived and wrangled with a local native rose locust (*Robinia neomexicana*), with similar benefits and similar drawbacks, in my own garden; I no longer consider it garden-worthy because of its aggressive root sprouting (think whack-a-mole with leaves). For erosion control on slopes and along seasonally flooding streams in the mountains, the locally native *Robinia* excels. Fast growth and tenacity are virtues in the right place and in the right proportion

with companions that can hold their own against the intrepid invasives. Aggressive growth, especially when it describes exotic plants overwhelming native species, is the dark side of tenacity. Planting choices were based on the ability to survive current conditions, adapt to increasing heat and limited water, and be easily managed where planted. Plants whose vices outnumbered their virtues were not considered for the updated gardens of Los Poblanos.

Salt cedar. *Tamarix chinensis* was introduced to New Mexico in the early 1900s for erosion control along streams and quickly adopted as an ornamental because of its feathery texture, long–blooming pale pink wisps of flowers on slender red stems, and adaptability under difficult growing conditions. This tree in the Greely Garden is one of the oldest in the valley. Photograph by the author.

A branch of salt cedar frames the top of this historic photo, confirmation that it was one of the earliest plantings. The fig that replaced the conical evergreen shown remains a productive element in the Greely Garden to this day. Gelatin silver print by Laura Gilpin, P1979.108.445.17, Amon Carter Museum of American Art, bequest of the artist.

One could write an entire book about salt cedar in the Southwest. Introduced in the early 1900s for erosion control along perennial and intermittent streams, it was adopted early as an ornamental because of its feathery texture, its long-blooming pale pink wisps of flowers on slender red stems, and its adaptability in difficult growing conditions. Within a generation, it proved to grow much too easily, whether cultivated or not, and in another generation it became a monster in need of serious control along waterways. Because salt cedar self-sows prolifically and, after disturbance, seedlings survive in places where natives are slower to recover, controls are still only marginally effective. Cursed for excessive water use, which research has shown is not generally true, salt cedar thrives in part by adapting to the moisture available and being extremely xeric when necessary—it is a model of resiliency in times of rapid climate change. It has also become habitat for the endangered willow flycatcher where native willows have died out because the consistent supply of shallow groundwater that willows require is no longer available. Salt cedar has usurped the willow's place because it adapts to drier soils when necessary. Salt cedar also provides a long season of pollen and nectar for both native and honeybees, which both bees and beekeepers appreciate, although honey made primarily from salt cedar has a rather rough taste, so it is generally blended with other, milder kinds of honey. The copper-red twigs of salt cedar are used in cabinetry trim work, and the larger stems make elegant weather-resistant fencing. Encouraging and managing the harvesting of the wood for these uses could help keep salt cedar in check while preserving its assets.

Doctors of oriental medicine value salt cedar as a chelator of heavy metals, while people wanting to control its spread curse it as adding mineral salts to already saline soils with its leaf litter. When conditions are extreme, it pays to weigh the plusses and minuses. Despite years of effort, tons of herbicides, and ground war to physically remove salt cedar from watersheds, only localized gains have been made to control its spread. More recently, beetles endemic to salt cedar's native habitats in Eurasia have been deployed to control it by repeated defoliation; the idea is to weaken the plant so that it becomes less invasive in native plant communities while establishing its specific biological control within those communities. This is the ongoing saga of good intentions sometimes overshadowed by problematic unintended consequences. Whether this latest biological control strategy will work, and whether the beetle will have an impact on the future of the (there is only one) salt cedar in the Greely Garden, is yet to be seen in this drama of plant adaptation.

The Garden Relationship between Los Poblanos Hacienda and La Quinta

From the south end of the patio, shaded from the strongest southern sun by golden raintree (*Koelreuteria paniculata*) and perfumed in early spring by burkwood viburnum (*V. × burkwoodii*), the path leads to the east–west walkway that separates La Quinta from the residence. One of three irrigation channels that divert water from the Griegos Lateral splits to parallel the walkway on both sides. This Acequia Medio—the middle irrigation channel that floods the lawn and border south of the residence, the hedge of eastern red cedar (*Juniperus virginiana*), and the lawn north of La Quinta—is shaded by native valley cottonwoods (*Populus deltoides* spp. *wislizeni*) and sycamores (*Platanus × acerifolia*).

A wide perennial bed borders the walkway on the residence side, and a narrower perennial border parallels the path in front of the tall juniper hedge on the La Quinta side. Lilacs (*Syringa*), peonies (*Paonia* cultivars), native golden columbine (*Aquilegia chrysantha*), daylilies (*Hemerocallis* cultivars), bearded irises (*Iris germanica* cultivars), tall summer phlox (*P. paniculata*), native pitcher sage (*Salvia azurea grandiflora*), goldenrod (*Solidago canadensis* spp. *gilvocanescens*), bundleflower (*Desmanthus illinoensis*), and Maximilian sunflower (*Helianthus maxilmiliani*) are among the perennials that make a stroll along that path welcoming throughout the seasons. The goldenrod and bundleflower are bosque natives and may have been introduced in the acequia water, an evolution of the camp followers in that they are volunteer species that are welcome as valuable pollinator support. The goldenrod also hosts the beneficial insects that parasitize thrips, a common rose pest, and the dried seedpods of bundleflower are an interesting addition to fall and winter dried bouquets. Urns that frame gateways are filled with seasonal flowers and replenished with conifer branches and bundles of decorative dried seed heads, so even in the dead of winter, the caring hands of the gardeners are evident. Footbridges over the acequia lead through gaps in the hedge to a flagstone path across the lawn to the formal north door of La Quinta, set in the middle of a symmetrical facade framed with a Greek revival pediment and pilasters. The juniper hedge obscures this formal entrance, which is now primarily used to access the north lawn during small events.

Guests of Ruth Simms entered La Quinta through an apple orchard and the east courtyard. This territorial revival building, sited in a former alfalfa field south of the residence, is grand in scale, designed as a community resource, and it elevates Los Poblanos Ranch from a fine farmstead to a country place. Intended as a public venue, it was called La Quinta, which translates from Spanish as "country place." Intentionally sited near the residence, the combined gardens transition into the larger landscape. The adjacent lawns serve as spaces for entertaining and are separated from the entrance driveway by a tall adobe wall with an ornate iron gate at the east end of the walkway. The acequia is piped under the entrance drive and is still used to irrigate the elm (*Ulmus pumila*) allée that shades the main driveway.

The Gardens of La Quinta

La Quinta's fifteen thousand square feet include a library, art gallery, ballroom, changing rooms for the pool, and guest rooms built in a U configuration facing east, framing Albuquerque's first swimming pool. The indoor spaces open onto the Grand Portal, which joins the gracious handcrafted interior to

The acequia–irrigated *Ulmus pumila* allée that shades the main driveway, autumn 2013. Even in winter, the sculptural arching branches and rugged, tessellated bark are features to admire. Siberian elms have stood sentinel here for ninety years but have fallen from favor in the Rio Grande watershed, largely because they rain down millions of papery seeds that germinate too well, so the trees are listed as a noxious weeds in New Mexico. Photograph by the author.

Entryway allée in spring 2018. In spring an understory of bridal wreath spirea (*Spirea prunifolia*) arches and spills along the drive until the tree canopy fills with leaves. At one time the understory was colored with masses of peonies (*Paonia* spp.), which still grow in the Greely Garden and along the north wall of La Quinta. In summer, the stately elms create a cool corridor, a welcoming approach. Photograph by the author.

outdoor spaces with similar wood doors carved by Gustave Baumann and with a fresco of San Ysidro, the patron saint of farmers, created by Peter Hurd. The archives at Los Poblanos contain 1937 correspondence between Hurd and Meem regarding the plaster surface for the mural. Meem's response revealed that the first coat was one part Portland cement to three parts sand, with ten pounds of hydrated lime per sack of cement. The final coat was one part Medusa or Atlas Portland cement, three parts clean sharp sand, and ten pounds of hydrated lime per sack of cement. The master craftsmen collaborated on a project that has weathered beautifully.

An example of Renaissance villa gardens characteristic of country places, the Grand Portal had a panoramic view across farm fields and desert grassland to the Sandia Mountains. Greely seems to have been enchanted by the "breathtaking yellows and blues of valley and mountain as a background, where you would not dare to introduce the contrasting green of the grass but use instead the blues and grays of native cactus, yuccas, and sagebrush." Thus she limited the lawn carpet around the swimming pool to a slim functional border and naturalized the vista in keeping with arts and crafts movement thinking. The space

This early photograph shows a corner of the Grand Portal at La Quinta a few years after it was first planted. Gelatin silver print by Laura Gilpin, P1979.108.445.9, Amon Carter Museum of American Art, bequest of the artist.

This detail from the new La Quinta site plan shows the gazebo garden between La Quinta and the Griegos Lateral acequia. The garden is little changed since the Simms era; the first swimming pool in Albuquerque is still prominent in the courtyard. On the terrace below the pool, the drawing shows rows of elms (*Ulmus parvifolia* 'Emer II') planted in 2009 in what was once an apple orchard. Graphic by Hannah Aulick and the author.

below the pool terrace has been reworked several times to serve changing times and uses, and there is little evidence of Greely's design there now.

The west garden of La Quinta includes a large gazebo-like covered patio immediately adjacent to the ballroom with a fireplace for chilly evenings. A strip of acequia-irrigated lawn runs along the length of the back wall of the building, and a boxwood parterre frames a silver maple (*Acer saccharinum*), a tree whose long life is witness to the

value of acequia irrigation on species that tend to succumb early to environmental stress in the high desert. A tall privet hedge encloses the pathway to the patio, and tall native pines (*Pinus ponderosa*) and dogwood (*Cornus cornuta*) screen this garden space from the Griegos Lateral. Given that ninety years have passed since Greely designed the gardens and Simms oversaw their construction and planting, the imprints of both women's styles remain to a surprising degree, likely because Greely balanced landscape architecture with horticulture and horticulture with plant ecology. Both women were dedicated to functionality, so the context of the site, a working southwestern farm and ranch, strongly influenced how the designed landscape fit into it.

The Gardens in Context

The gardens did not dominate the larger landscape they occupied; they transitioned into it seamlessly or were enclosed by walls to buffer exotic plants from the elements. Shaded living spaces—some intimate and private, others grand in scale to accommodate outdoor entertaining on an equally grand scale—were enclosed by hedges or walls, while key viewsheds were open to magnificent panoramas. The surrounding agricultural landscape has since been suburbanized, displacing the vast expanse of desert and mountains that Greely would have perceived as the context of her design. The vastly broader horizons of New Mexico were unfamiliar ground for her primarily eastern experience. She carefully worked to complement the buildings' regional architecture and to link indoor entertainment spaces with gracious outdoor adjuncts, deftly blending locally native plants with regional natives and adapted exotics by carefully placing them in their preferred niches.

The gardens transitioned from formal planting surrounding La Quinta into farm fields to the south and east. A sunken cutting and kitchen garden on the north side of the residence was separated from the dairy and working ranch by a grape and gourd arbor that separated the garden on the west side from the Griegos Acequia. On the north

border, the Lord and Burnham greenhouse, which Simms used for propagating roses and breeding new varieties of mums (*Chrysanthemum* cultivars), was intended to expand the local market. The greenhouse, originally glass, has been restored twice and was recently re-covered in clear twin-wall polycarbonate plastic. It is still well used today for propagating lavender and growing vegetable and flower crops through winter. Several outbuildings were associated with this part of the gardens: a potting shed, wine pressing house, and adjacent wine cellar. East of these were two parallel buildings: the milking barns and sales room for the Albuquerque Dairy Co-op, which later became Creamland Dairies. The iconic silos are just south of these barns, no longer used to store feed but structurally sound and eventually to be repurposed, perhaps as a distillery.

The Simmses experimented with new varieties of crops, and expanded and certified dairy production as the growth of Albuquerque increased demand. The marriage of Albert and Ruth joined his purebred Guernsey herd—high butterfat and protein producers—with her prized Holstein-Friesians—high-volume milk producers—from her farm in Illinois. Her Rock River Farm in Byron, Illinois, had been a model in the production of certified milk, Holstein-Friesian cattle, and alfalfa (*Medicago sativa*). At Los Poblanos they experimented with new strains of alfalfa to feed the livestock and produced sugar beet seeds (*Beta vulgaris*) in an effort to reduce their reliance on inconsistent supplies of seeds and imported sugar during wartime. They used turkeys as biocontrol for grasshoppers and also bred churro sheep, an ancient Iberian breed introduced by the Spanish in the 1500s.

Churro sheep are well adapted to climate extremes, having a top coat of long-staple fleece and a soft undercoat. The fleece is valued for its luster,

Churro sheep are well adapted to climate extremes. The fleece is valued for its luster, silky texture, and durability and is part of the traditional textile weaving of Native peoples in New Mexico. The meat is considered superior in flavor and low in fat, a characteristic that gives it currency at Los Poblanos today. Photograph by Wes Brittenham.

silky texture, and durability and is part of the traditional textile weaving of Native peoples in New Mexico. The meat is considered superior in flavor and low in fat, characteristics that gives it currency at Los Poblanos today. While this discussion might seem beyond the realm of ornamental gardens, the divide between gardening for beauty and food farming is rather blurry. As a landscape design style, the *ferme ornee* movement of about 1740 to 1820 set a precedent for the fusion of producing farms with ornamental gardens. The integration of pleasure gardens with farmland and kitchen garden was in practice as early as Roman villas and was formalized in the literature in the 1730s by Stephen

Switzer. In colonial America, ferme ornee was favored by both Thomas Jefferson and Andrew Jackson Downing. Nearly a century later, Downing's ideas about the social merit of home food production and orderly, planned garden design were in evidence at Los Poblanos; they are still seen in the gardens today.

While the gardens grew and were enjoyed by increasing numbers of guests, including those who were wined and dined as community benefactors, and artists who were entertained for their stimulating company and their contributions to the beauty of Los Poblanos, Ruth Simms was increasingly drawn into community affairs. She may have temporarily abandoned national politics, but she had skills to exercise locally. Albuquerque was a growing town of thirty-five thousand in the 1930s, unsophisticated by her standards but poised on the verge of broader horizons. Her first project was founding a school for her youngest daughter, Bazy, in 1932. The Sandia School for Girls was intended to tutor Bazy and the daughters of a few good friends, to transition them to eastern prep schools and later to colleges. By 1936 Bazy was away at school in the East, but the demand for college preparatory education for girls was evident: the Sandia School had expanded to seventy-five students in grades 1 through 10, and Simms was enmeshed in building plans for a space to accommodate them.

Investing both her money and her time, she again worked with John Gaw Meem on designing the campus, located near the Parkland-Ridgecrest addition in Southeast Albuquerque. For the project, Simms continued to engage locally and more widely known artists, as she had done at La Quinta. She was a one-woman Depression-era relief program for little-known artists of promise. Because she had the foresight and the organizational skills, and she made the time, Simms also used her Washington

Ruth Simms (right) enlisted John Gaw Meem to design a campus for her Sandia Girls School and commissioned sculptor Eugenie Shonnard (left) to create *Youth in the Desert*. Gelatin silver print by Laura Gilpin, circa 1941, P1979.102.47, Amon Carter Museum of American Art, bequest of the artist.

ily, friends, and neighbors. In Katherine Sargeant and Mary Davis's 1986 oral history of the North Valley, *Shining River, Precious Land*, Ann Simms Clark, the Simmses' niece and next door neighbor, remembered her aunt and the parties at Los Poblanos: "Two parties stand out in my memory. They had a ranch in Colorado, the Trinchera Ranch, and there were buffalo up there in one of the high mountain parks, and the Forest Service people said that the buffalo must be eliminated from that park, and they gave some to zoos, but not every zoo wanted buffalo, and finally, it came down to the fact that they slaughtered one of them and we had buffalo meat at one of those parties. It was delicious because it's grass-fed meat." This party-related recollection underscores the Simmses' practical agrarian way of turning a problem—surplus bison—into a social event, introducing new foods while savoring the company of family and friends.

Clark also recalled that "her daughters had a surprise party for my Aunt Ruth, and they gave her—this was one of the early days—they gave her a little Sicilian donkey as a present, and they brought the donkey in with bells around his neck and ribbons. . . . You know it was a little, little thing and they named the donkey 'Angelino' and it was taken down to Manzano Day School, and every year when they did the Christmas pageant, Angelino would carry the Virgin, so he became very well acquainted with lots of children."

And to emphasize that the Simms parties were occasions large and small: "But there were lots of parties there and she loved to play poker, and she had a poker table there, to the consternation of the wives of some of the old-time doctors and others. She had a poker game going every couple of weeks."

In the same oral history, ranch hand J. R. Kitts remembered the annual fall barbecue at La Quinta, when ranch work eased up. Kitts worked for Albert

connections to secure approval of the Albuquerque Little Theater as the first WPA project in the city, garnering communitywide financial support. She became the second Little Theater board president in 1937. She was also a member of the Museum of New Mexico board of regents, and because of her appreciation for the work of Native American artists, she served on the managing board of the School of American Research. The gardens of Los Poblanos were the setting for much of the entertaining that galvanized community support for the arts and education.

The entertaining also included extended fam-

Simms for many years and estimated that in 1938–1939, Los Poblanos Ranch had a herd of four hundred dairy cattle, fifteen hundred sheep, and some beef cattle that grazed on the old Elena Gallegos Grant Land. He remembered driving the stock from the farm in the valley up to the foothills in the spring and back in the fall—a distance of seven or eight miles—along what is now Osuna Road. As Albuquerque grew, herding cross-country was no longer possible, so the stock was hauled by truck. Kitts recalled, "I think there were around twenty-five families who worked on the ranch at one time. It was quite a farm. There were around 1,200 acres of farmland there and it took a lot of people to take care of it. There were eleven boys working the dairy."

Politics, Loss, and the End of a Golden Age in the Gardens

Politics was too important to both Simms to put it aside indefinitely. Ruth was respected for her political savvy and her ability to engage an audience. She worked to recoup the progress women had made politically before the Depression, and she actively encouraged women to seek office. Although fearing that Franklin Roosevelt was pushing the country toward socialism and that she would be considered an isolationist regarding war, she was much more socially progressive than Albert, likely because she was empathetic and enjoyed people so much. Her exposure to progressive movements in her role as a major national leader for women's suffrage added depth to her thinking on social issues. Ruth has been described as gracious and warm, easy to laugh with, and not afraid of hard work or plain talk, but she was raised in the political elite and could also appear aristocratic and aloof if it served her purposes. Albert was described as remote and chilly in

demeanor at times. He seemed to truly appreciate and yet be repeatedly surprised by his wife's skills, not unlike many husbands of the era.

The year 1938 was pivotal in the Simmses' lives. To expand their grazing capacity, and possibly to give Ruth's son from her first marriage, John Medill McCormick, a career option while he pursued his aspirations as a writer, Ruth sold her Rock River Farm in Illinois. The Simms then bought Trinchera Ranch, a 171,400-acre intact remnant of the Sangre de Cristo Land Grant in southern Colorado. By midsummer of that year, John McCormick had died in a fall while climbing on the precipitous west face of the Sandia Mountains. She could see the jagged rocky mountainside that had claimed her son from her windows at Los Poblanos, and his death seemed to steal the joy from her life. Focusing once again on politics was a distraction and a means of pulling herself out of despair. She first retreated to Trinchera Ranch but soon after returned to New Mexico to help in the gubernatorial campaign of a rancher friend, Albert Mitchell. Despite breaking her leg in a fall a few days before she was scheduled to give a radio address, she gave that speech in support of the Republican ticket in New Mexico from her hospital bed. At the same time, throwing her energy into community education, she also founded Manzano Day School, first housed at Castle Huning and later moved across Central Avenue to the first Huning hacienda, where it remains today. The original hacienda is surrounded by modern school facilities and continues to provide premier early childhood education.

By late 1939 Ruth Simms was well enough physically and emotionally to mentor the crusading prosecutor and later governor of New York, Thomas Dewey, in his presidential bid against Franklin Roosevelt. She was named comanager of Dewey's preconvention campaign, called

"Headman of the Dewey Brain Trust" and "Generalissima'am" by both supporters and critics, who grudgingly respected her abilities despite the fact that she was female. The gardens of Los Poblanos were likely again the setting for gatherings to support her candidate. Dewey lost the primary but gained prestige in the Republican Party, partly because of his association with her. Simms returned to Los Poblanos and her work at Sandia School. Soon, citing problems at Trinchera Ranch as a reason to again leave Los Poblanos, she went north to run the ranch in support of the war effort and to fill the gap in ranch hands there with her own determined physical labor. By the next campaign cycle, Simms's relationship with Dewey had soured. Dewey was not appreciative of Ruth's forthright advice, and he feared her increasingly unpopular isolationist views. Simms was not capable of allowing what she saw as his political gaffes to undermine his career. Then, due to its proximity to Kirtland Air Force Base, the Sandia School campus was requisitioned for wartime use as a military hospital. Simms once again dedicated herself to improving conditions at Trinchera Ranch.

Albert Simms remained enmeshed in local politics, business, and ranching obligations in New Mexico. The considerable maintenance of the gardens intermittently required forty or more workers. Ironically, during World War II, German prisoners of war were employed to temporarily fill the ranks of local men who were fighting abroad. English gardener and landscape architect Cecil Pragnell, who had worked on the grounds at the Hearst Castle at San Simeon, had been brought to Los Poblanos by Ruth Simms to work with Rose Greely. He bought the historic mill on John Simms's neighboring property and renovated it as his home. Pragnell may have planned and planted the one hundred–tree apple orchard in the pasture

east of La Quinta and is remembered as a man as genial as he was skilled. He was county extension agent at the time when POW labor was offered to offset the lack of local manpower, and he helped facilitate the prisoner workforce. Albert Simms, then chairman of the board of commissioners of the Middle Rio Grande Conservancy District, was allocated fifteen POWs as farm labor at Los Poblanos.

In October 1944, Ruth Simms was riding the range doing routine ranch work at Trinchera when her horse stepped in a hole and faltered. She landed on a rock on her shoulder and broke bones, a complex injury that required surgery at a Chicago hospital. She spent time convalescing in the hospital during, for Republicans, a losing presidential campaign that likely hurt Ruth as much as the fractures. Within days of leaving the hospital, she was readmitted in terrible pain and diagnosed with hemorrhagic pancreatitis, bleeding in or around a ruptured pancreas. She died a few weeks later, at the very end of 1944, at sixty-four years of age. She finally returned to Los Poblanos accompanied by her husband and her daughters and was interred in Fairview Park Cemetery in Albuquerque.

After Ruth's untimely death, Albert Simms continued to run Los Poblanos Ranch as headquarters for their vast property holdings, gradually selling off parcels as the postwar suburbanization that was typical across the United States swallowed up farmland in Albuquerque's North Valley. Given the plantings that have survived since the 1930s, through the severe drought that gripped the Southwest from 1942 until 1956, Albert Simms must have maintained the status quo, with gardeners continuing to irrigate the hacienda and La Quinta landscapes and the dairy and ranch pastures. But the golden age of the gardens of Los Poblanos seems to have stalled with the accidental death of young

A WPA-style panel series painted by Harry Garrison Miller on the wall of the Grand Portal tells the story of farming and ranching at Los Poblanos. It was added in 1951, many years after the nearby Hurd mural of San Ysidro was created.

John McCormick in 1938. Active experimenting in the greenhouses, rose breeding, and growing cutting gardens had been Ruth's domain, and they all must have languished with her passing. The interest and spirit behind them were gone. Albert outlived Ruth by twenty years. He was said to be much less gregarious than his wife, so the gardens of Los Poblanos likely saw fewer public events in the years after her death, except perhaps for the much celebrated end-of-season barbecues in the barn and parklike gardens; the Christmas celebrations for the ranch hands, the farmers, and their families, friends, and neighbors; and the occasional Republican party fundraiser.

Neighbors remember Albert fondly. The young Anella brothers, whose parents bought the John Simms estate south of Los Poblanos, loved riding their bikes up and down the shaded elm allée next door in summer. Anthony Anella, an architect with an Aldo Leopold–inspired land ethic and coauthor of *Saving the Ranch: Conservation Easement Design in the American West*, was four years old when his family moved next door to "Uncle Albert" at Los Poblanos. He remembers frequent Sunday morning coffees with his father and Simms, nearly a ritual in the neighborhood. Anella summarized their relationship by recasting a well-known aphorism: "There's that old saying: good fences make good neighbors. Well, I think there's another: good gates make good neighbors." Albert built a gate in the fence between the Anellas and Los Poblanos and painted on it "Toney's [*sic*] Gate," so his young neighbors could enjoy Los Poblanos without the danger of riding out on Rio Grande Boulevard. Anella remembers the orchard as having the best Winesap apples he has ever eaten.

Heritage apple tree. Through the 1950s and 1960s, an apple orchard of more than 130 trees occupied the terrace east of La Quinta, running halfway to Rio Grande Boulevard. This is one of the only surviving trees from that orchard, still producing excellent fruit. Photograph by the author.

The Simms Legacy

Putting the 1942 to 1956 drought period of farming and ranching in perspective, in 1946 there were sixty thousand acres of irrigated farmland in the Middle Rio Grande Valley. Two-thirds of those farms had fewer than fifteen acres. Of the remaining third, Simms owned two of the largest operations. Los Poblanos, the original home of Creamland Dairies, was only one of them; Hope Farms in Socorro was the alternate pasturage.

Trinchera, the heritage ranch in southern Colorado purchased when Ruth Simms sold her farm in Illinois, was summer grazing for more livestock. Accounts of numbers of cattle and sheep grazed, as well as dairy cows milked by hand (not using the new mechanized equipment that could injure breeding stock and required round-the-clock milking shifts) lead me to make a few assumptions. The land Albert Simms stewarded was well taken care of, and he kept himself and crews of experienced ranch hands, field farmers, shepherds, and milkers gainfully employed. A rancher in Sierra County of south-central New Mexico once told me that with land value what it is, a man would have to be a fool to abuse land he owned. He said that most of the overgrazing in the Southwest was on public land leased for ridiculously low fees that did not cover adequate oversight of the leases. Certainly, Albert Simms was no fool. It costs more upfront to steward the land, but Simms held the long view.

I base the good stewardship assumption on the fact that Los Poblanos desert grassland, the eastern portion of the former Elena Gallegos Land Grant, had been erratically managed, degraded by drought, and heavily used prior to the Simmses acquiring it. The rotating of stock recalled in the oral histories would have helped it recover somewhat but would have limited its carrying capacity, especially given the intense drought. Irrigated alfalfa and grain and alternate pasturage supplemented grazing. Trinchera Ranch had been in prime condition when Ruth and Albert Simms purchased it and has since become a conservation easement US Fish and Wildlife–protected habitat and migration corridor, valued for its continuous management in pristine condition. The Simmses valued land and understood how to manage land and livestock respectfully and profitably.

Ruth Simms was the driving force behind the creation of Los Poblanos and La Quinta and the gardens that surround them. In just over a decade, she also founded Manzano Day School and Sandia School, and her contributions to the Albuquerque Little Theater changed the city forever. Together the Simms had succeeded in reassembling much of the Elena Gallegos Land Grant and returning it to agricultural use. Toward the end of his life, Albert maintained the twenty-five acres of valley farmland that continues as Los Poblanos. He endowed the Albuquerque Academy with much of the ranch land, which was then sold to the city of Albuquerque and Cibola National Forest effectively preserving the foothills as open space for a rapidly growing community.

As the valley became increasingly suburban, people were drawn by the tall trees and meandering acequias, the lushness that proximity to the Rio Grande provides. Paradoxically, development eroded the sense of place that drew the new homeowners. Sprinkler-irrigated lawns displaced acequia-irrigated farm fields and the shallow water table began to drop below the level that supported the cottonwood canopy. Some descendants of early settlers were dismissive of the patron relationship, and of the wealth they saw as gained by their losses. Surely there were tax advantages in Simmses' generosity, but business acumen was balanced by a family history of valuing and supporting education, in keeping the land agricultural and thereby preserving the cultural values of the middle Rio Grande Valley. The story of the unease generated by change, friction between tradition and progress, and the conflict between the common good and personal profit and loss is as old as humankind.

The reach of the Simms legacy continued as Sandia Prep and Albuquerque Academy both developed environmental science curricula to engender a love of nature in future generations. Much of the campus of the academy is an undeveloped open space that serves as a wildlife habitat and outdoor study space in the middle of suburban Albuquerque. In addition, the academy developed a Desert Oasis Teaching Garden to give students and the community the opportunity to explore practices for regenerative agriculture, water conservation, and adaptation to climate change.

The influence of Los Poblano also imprinted on generations closer to home. Albert Simms III, a grandnephew of Albert Simms, received an extracurricular education at Los Poblanos. Now a Taos attorney and an amateur steward of heirloom apple trees, he told me in correspondence. "I did work on the farm crew [at Los Poblanos] starting age thirteen, in 1957, for a few years." He noted that "a fellow Pilar resident, Abran Archuleta . . . told me he worked on the garden crew [at Los Poblanos] during the '50s." Simms purchased his property in Pilar from Abran's uncle Matias Archuleta. He continued, "There is a five-acre orchard of fifty- to hundred-year-old apple trees, some of which I have managed to identify as famous heirloom varieties. The thought occurred to me that the apple orchard in front of La Quinta may have been planned by a knowledgeable pomologist and that Abran may have brought cuttings of scion wood back to Matias to graft into the orchard here in Pilar."

One of the apple trees at Los Poblanos remains at the edge of the current farm fields. It is entirely possible, in the small gardening world that is New Mexico, that Albert Simms III is tending the legacy of trees planted under the aegis of his grand-uncle.

Sources, and an Invitation to Dig Deeper

Anella, Anthony, and John B. Wright. *Saving the Ranch: Conservation Easement Design in the American West*. Washington, DC: Island Press, 2004.

Birnbaum, Charles A., and Robin Karson. *Pioneers of American Landscape Design*, Vol. 2. New York: McGraw-Hill, 2000.

Brunt, Charles D. "Family Connection: Simms Family." *Albuquerque Journal*, January 27, 2015, https://www.pressreader.com/usa/albuquerque-journal/20150127/283695477944076.

Doyle, Susan Badger. "German and Italian Prisoners of War in Albuquerque, 1943–1946." *New Mexico Historical Review* 66, no. 3 (1991), https://digitalrepository.unm.edu/cgi/viewcontent.cgi?article=2929&context=nmhr.

Lawson, Joanne Seale. "Remarkable Foundations, Rose Ishbel Greely, Landscape Architect." *Washington History* 10, no. 1 (Spring/Summer 1998): 46–69.

Miller, Kristie. *Ruth Hanna McCormick: A Life in Politics 1880–1944*. Albuquerque: University of New Mexico Press, 1992.

North Valley Oral History Project, Center for Southwest Research, Zimmerman Library, University of New Mexico, Albuquerque.

Sargeant, Kathryn, and Mary Davis. *Shining River, Precious Land: An Oral History of Albuquerque's North Valley*. Albuquerque: Albuquerque Museum, 1986.

Scurlock, Dan. "From the Rio to the Sierra: An Environmental History of the Middle Rio Grande Basin." US Forest Service, 1998, https://www.fs.usda.gov/treesearch/pubs/5133.

Taylor, Phyllis. "Albuquerque's Environmental Story: Educating for a Sustainable Community." Friends of Albuquerque's Environmental Story, 2008, https://albuqhistsoc.org/aes/s2nalb.html.

University of Virginia Library. "A Guide to the Rose Greely Architectural Drawings and Papers, 1909–1961." Archival Resources of

the Virginias, https://ead.lib.virginia.edu/
vivaxtf/view?docId=uva-sc/viu01527.xml,
accessed November 3, 2022.

University of New Mexico Medical Center Library Oral History Project. "Interview with Albert G. Simms II, MD." New Mexico Digital Collections, 1984, https://nmdigital.unm.edu/digital/collection/nmhhc/id/188/.

Van Citters, Karen. *A Brief History of Urban Trees in New Mexico*. USDA Forest Service, January 15, 2018, https://groundworkstudionm.com/wp-content/uploads/2019/06/A-Brief-History-of-Urban-Trees-in-NM.pdf.

Weideman, Paul. "Meem's Meme: Los Poblanos." *Pasatiempo*, September 19, 2014.

Wilson, Chris. *Facing Southwest: The Life and Houses of John Gaw Meem*. New York: W. W. Norton, 2002.

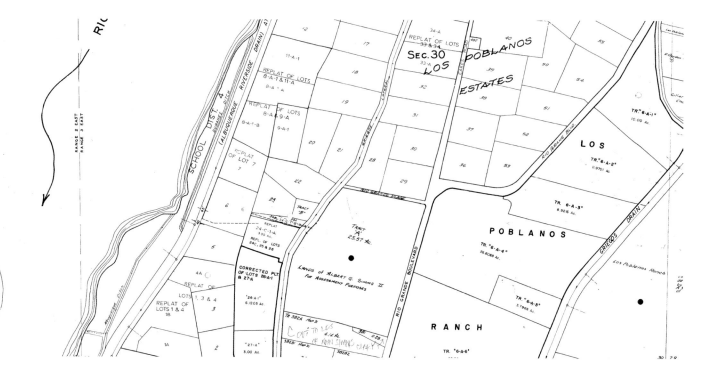

Map showing the transfer of land to Albert G. Simms II and the ongoing subdivision of Los Poblanos Ranch lands into suburban parcels.

CHAPTER 4

The Private Family Gardens of Los Poblanos and the Return to Community, 1965-2004

Querencia is a place where one feels safe, a place from which one's strength of character is drawn, where one feels at home.
—*Juan Esteban Arellano, farmer, historian, poet*

Toward the end of Albert Simms I's life, Los Poblanos Ranch shrank from twelve hundred acres of farmland worked by twenty-five families in Simms's employ to the present twenty-five acres. Soon after his death, the estate passed into the caring hands of his favorite nephew, Albert G. Simms II, a respected general surgeon and community leader, and his wife, Barbara. They continued fostering education with their decades-long support of the Albuquerque Academy and Sandia Preparatory School. Over four decades the Simms family had an enormously beneficial impact on the city of Albuquerque as it became a cosmopolitan urban center but the era of extensive farming and ranching was over. Within a few years, the dairy at Los Poblanos closed and Los Poblanos continued as the Simms family residence starting in 1968. According Mary Field Simms, her parents considered Los Poblanos as simply their family home. They celebrated hol-

idays, weddings, and all things family there. Her paternal grandmother lived just down the boulevard and came for supper almost every night. Her parents loved the community and supported it in many ways, but their family home was a place for their personal time together.

Though Barbara Simms loved to entertain and had beautiful parties for family and friends, the gatherings were on a smaller scale than Ruth Simms's La Quinta galas. Mary Simms recalled her father as a busy general surgeon who even made house calls. Dr. Simms would get home just in time to greet guests at gatherings master-planned by Barbara. Among Barbara Simms's extrafamilial annual events were tea parties in honor of the graduating seniors of Sandia School (now Sandia Preparatory School).

To say that the Simmses were committed to their community is a bit of an understatement and perhaps a genetic inevitability. Neither Sandia

Preparatory School nor Albuquerque Academy would likely have become the educational institutions they are today without the Simmses' personal interest and continued financial support. Barbara was pivotal in reviving Ruth Simms's Sandia Girls School and transforming it into its present coed, sixth-through-twelfth-grade form, Sandia Prep.

Mary Simms's further recalled her childhood: "The joy and love of gardening were lifelong for both my parents." Albert was the forester in the family, planting trees, while Barbara "was our flower power. She was a meticulous gardener, never a weed in sight, and always a bounty of blooms with her green thumb. Her gardens were spectacular." During the growing season, Barbara filled the family home with beautiful floral arrangements. She consulted with Rosalie Doolittle on rose and peony selections for her Los Poblanos garden. Doolittle was an esteemed local gardener; a consulting rosarian for the Albuquerque Rose Society, of which she was a founding member in 1948; and was also coauthor with Harriet Tiedebohl of *Southwest Gardening*. At one time the main entrance drive at Los Poblanos was lined with peonies (*Paeonia* spp.) under the elm canopy.

According to the 1980 Los Poblanos District National Register of Historic Places inventory nomination form, the only major change in the landscaping of Los Poblanos since Albert and Ruth Simms's day was the large lagoon east of the hacienda, which was added in the 1960s by Dr. Simms and his son Frank. Mary Simms recalled visiting Lucia Batten's gardens at Batten House nearby. Lucia Batten had invited Barbara and the Simms children to explore the pond and to enjoy the ducks and geese there. The seed was planted, and the pond at Los Poblanos was dug. As Frank Simms related in a recent letter, "I have lots of memories of the Los Poblanos Ranch, which was quite an extensive farming and ranching operation. The Holstein Friesian dairy herd, milk parlor, Clydesdale teams pulling feed wagons, haybarns, grain mill, grain silos, corn bins, sheep, hogs, chickens, orchards, alfalfa fields, milo fields, all the farm equipment you could imagine, greenhouses, gardens, irrigators, gardeners, blacksmiths, ranch hands, and the duck pond which I built. All conspired to make growing up there a magical experience."

Mary Simms summarized her life at Los Poblanos in warm and generous terms, also using the word *magical* to describe her childhood. The valley was truly rural, and Los Poblanos was surrounded by farm fields. The children enjoyed "playing in the barn, the haystacks, the silos, climbing the apple trees, riding horses and so much more that comes from country living."

Time passes, life progresses, and a new chapter in family history is written. After a decade of living at Los Poblanos, with their children grown, Sandia Prep well established, the Albuquerque Academy thriving, and after thirty-four years of rigorous surgical practice, Barbara and Albert Simms II decided to sell the property so they could travel and enjoy a more leisurely life. Barbara found an apt successor in both the love of gardening and floral flair in Penny Rembe. Armin Rembe and his brother-in-law Robert Walker shared a penchant for tree planting with Dr. Simms.

The Rembe and Walker Era: Gentleman Farming Returns 1978-2004

The Rembes at Los Poblanos

The Rembes had been living in another John Gaw Meem–designed home, the Lovelace House, in the Southeast Heights of Albuquerque when they

The pond was initially dug by Frank Simms, who was inspired by the pond at Batten House. From its inception, it has been a draw for migratory and resident waterfowl and a lesson in wetland ecology for curious children and adults. Photograph by the author

learned that Los Poblanos was on the market. It was an opportunity too exceptional to let pass by, especially since much of the land at Los Poblanos would likely be subdivided and sold as suburban lots if they did nothing to intervene. With the Walkers (Armin's sister Victoria and her husband, Robert), they could preserve the historic buildings and keep the land rural. In 1978 the Simms estate was divided in two and a new family dynasty assumed stewardship of Los Poblanos. Penny and Armin Rembe bought the north half of the estate: Los Poblanos Ranch with the original Simms

hacienda, Greely Garden, greenhouse, and barn. The Walkers purchased La Quinta and adjacent gardens. Together with parenting their young families, the Rembes and Walkers maintained careers that might have been engrossing enough for less garden-inspired people, but they dove into country life with enthusiasm.

Armin Rembe, a respected oncologist-hematologist, the first in Albuquerque, added "Farmin' Armin" to an already impressive résumé. He became an amateur beekeeper, maintaining several top bar hives, and began a large organic

Many decades after the placita gardens were planted, the Moorish fountain continues to refresh with its water music. Planting has evolved to include a drapery of Lady Banks roses, which over time have become signature plants in the gardens of Los Poblanos. Photograph by the author.

garden. He brought the vegetables he harvested there to La Montañita Co-op on his way to the hospital. Penny worked to restore the estate's historic flower gardens while she volunteered with the Junior League and developed several businesses. Pennysmith's Paper sold quality paper, stationery, event invitations, and gifts. Valley Deli specialized in gourmet foods not commonly available in the city at the time, and the New Mexico Catalog featured a collection of unique offerings, including a specially blended paint the color of the New Mexico sky. Penny also later served on the board of regents at the University of New

Mexico. Ruth Simms and Rose Greely had set a high bar, and Barbara Simms had continued the legacy. Penny graciously and capably assumed the mantle of stewardship worn so elegantly by the women of Los Poblanos before her.

Emily Rembe recalls her mother's fingers stained with aphid juice from wiping the insects off tender rosebuds. Like mother, like daughter, one of Emily's own enduring chores, possibly not her favorite, was aphid patrol. She also helped at Pennysmith's and learned that business early on. A large part of the Rembe children's upbringing involved time outdoors, both unmonitored exploration and chores. Penny recalls a big sign on Rio Grande Boulevard: "Farmin' Armin's Organic Vegetables." The kids sold produce, an entrepreneurial experience that would serve them all well in adulthood. Matt Rembe has described his childhood as a "Huck Finn life." Jay Rembe remembers his childhood as a time of exploration with his siblings and cousins next door. Tending the farm animals, riding the acequia trails, and helping irrigate and rebuild aging fences—this work was fun.

In short order, a menagerie of livestock took up residence at Los Poblanos. Penny Rembe came from a ranching family that straddled the Texas–New Mexico border. Her father ranched near Amarillo and also ran a cow-calf operation on the Plains of San Agustin, south and west of Albuquerque. Grandfather Taylor gave each of his grandchildren a Chincoteague pony to ride and groom. These ponies are the wild stock, perhaps the survivors of a shipwrecked Spanish galleon, that have been conserved and have thrived on the barrier islands off the Maryland–Virginia coast. Every year the herd is culled of enough ponies to protect the ecological balance on the island, and proceeds of the sales pay for feed and veterinary care for the remaining animals and also support the local fire department. The resilient ponies forage salt grass, an advantage for those introduced to New Mexico since its soils and therefore its forage is higher in mineral salts than are the soils of most wetter climate pastures. The ponies likely found their match in the Rembe children, with great adventures and only a few broken bones.

When you have the land, the curiosity, four children, and a generous heart, "pets" tend to follow you home, so other animal adoptions followed. Choices of farm-mates are honed by experience, and the Suffolk sheep originally part of the Rembe menagerie were replaced with churro sheep, a return to the early Simms-era experimentation with the well-adapted breed. Soon pigs became part of the ensemble, Then guinea fowl, fun-to-watch polka dot–feathered birds (and living security alarms with their staccato vocalizations), and chickens for homegrown eggs joined the farm. A white peacock, aptly named Albert, was adopted from the Lucia Batten estate when the Albuquerque Museum Foundation inherited the Batten property and the foundation found itself heir to an ostentation of peafowl. Penny Rembe had been helping sort and catalog the contents of Batten House, and adoptions of the birds were hastily arranged to reduce their numbers. Los Poblanos was an obvious new habitat opportunity.

The gardens that she now stewarded were a great concern of Penny's. Her eighth-grade career ambition had been to have a greenhouse, and now

A white peacock, aptly named Albert, was adopted from the Lucia Batten estate when the Albuquerque Museum Foundation inherited the Batten property and found itself heir to an ostentation of peafowl. Photograph by the author.

she did. An avid gardener, surveying the responsibility she had undertaken, she understood the scope of work and contacted Marie Torrens for advice. Torrens was the force behind the Albuquerque Council of Garden Clubs' garden center, which hosts garden club events and is also rented out as a beautifully landscaped place to host weddings and other events. Supremely organized, business-savvy, and a gardener to the core, Torrens was the person to appeal to for help. While she could not directly put spade to soil, she did the next best thing: she sent Robert Squires, landscape architect and plantsman, to Penny Rembe's aid. Penny recalls that "Robert Squires worked here for quite a long time and did a lot of restoration in the gardens and fountains. Carmen Lucero was a holdover from the Simms family when we moved here. He was an expert irrigator." Lucero trained a succession of irrigators, including Robert Squires and Jesus Dominguez, to maintain the acequia tradition at Los Poblanos. To honor his memory, the sculpture of San Ysidro on the north edge of the pond today holds Lucero's hoe.

Armin Rembe expected his children to spend their time constructively—studying, tending animals, and engaging in activities that interested them on the farm. Jay Rembe remembers the farm and gardens as a playground. Growing up in buildings of timeless grace surrounded by rich farmland and gardens, and working with Robert Squires on renovating and planting projects in the gardens, sounds like an ideal initiation to one's lifework. Matt Rembe went on to find a means of preserving historic architecture, art, and landscape, while Jay Rembe found his forte in developing commercial, residential, and mixed-use urban infill projects that are respectful of the history of the places they complete. Matt and Jay worked with Robert Squires on mucking out the pond and restoring acequia irrigation to the Greely Garden. The clay tile channels were by then buried in silt and needed careful clearing to carry acequia water through the garden beds. Matt recalls the mixed blessing that that project entailed: the floodwater brought in weed seeds, which grew in the rose and peony beds and required additional work to control.

Squires had a fundamental weed control strategy, which Penny Rembe agreed with wholeheartedly: the way to minimize weeds is to limit their access to soil, light, and water by filling space densely with desirable plants, mostly perennials to avoid repeatedly disturbing the soil to replant. Penny began to grow perennials from seed and cuttings in the Los Poblanos greenhouse because they were not commonly supplied by local nurseries at the time. Squires was my introduction to Los Poblanos. He invited me to see what he was doing in the Greely Garden beds, which then were planted with grandiflora and tea rose varieties that produce huge flowers on tall, stout canes. Squires had planted medium-size and tall perennials such as 'Coronation Gold' yarrow (*Achillea filipendulina*), pitcher sage (*Salvia azurea grandiflora*), summer phlox (*P. paniculata*), and goldenrod (*Solidago canadensis*), with annuals such as cosmos (*C. bipinnatus*) and signet marigolds (*Tagetes tenuifolia*) to hide the ungainly rose canes while highlighting their flowers. These companions also extended the color show and attracted beneficial insects and songbirds. Since the infill plants were less thirsty than roses, most of the water continued to support the roses. The strong framework of the pathways helped make visual sense of the riot of colors and textures.

The lagoon built east of the hacienda during Dr. Simms's tenure was fenced by the Rembes to exclude coyotes so that the pond could be used by the Rio Grande Zoo in its recovery program for

The present–day lotus pond has evolved over time but remains a rare year–round water source for resi–dent and migratory waterfowl and many other wetland species. Photograph by the author.

endangered wildfowl species when Frank Hibben was zoo director. Hibben, at the Rembes' invitation, brought black swans and several small, shy bird species that were not successfully breeding at the zoo to the more tranquil environment at Los Poblanos. After the experiment ended, the fence was removed and the pond was mucked out and restored. Establishing peacocks to patrol the gardens of Los Poblanos was a lasting contribution from Hibben. Among Squires's contributions while he managed the gardens were four lotuses (*Nelumbo nucifera*) planted in the pond. From iso-

lated spots on one side of the lagoon, they spread to cover most of the water surface, producing beautiful blooms and reducing evaporation from the water surface.

At the time he tended the gardens of Los Poblanos, Squires was the father of three small children. They sometimes accompanied him to work and were invited to explore the gardens. Los Poblanos continued to grow as a place that nourishes family and inspires with plants. Penny and Armin Rembe were drawn to Los Poblanos in part by the Meem architecture but also by the land itself. They wanted their children to have space outdoors to become self-sufficient. This desire to let nature educate the next generation included livestock chores for the Rembe children: Jay and Armin tended the sheep, Matt tended the chickens and pigs, while Emily tended roses and helped in the shop. The nature studies extended well beyond the immediate family and soon Los Poblanos was hosting 4-H members, teaching through experience with piglets and goat kids, and showing children where their food comes from, how agriculture is science, and that science is fun.

The Walkers at La Quinta

Robert Walker, the new steward of La Quinta, also owned Treeland Nursery on the corner of Edith Boulevard and Osuna Road, at the eastern edge of Albuquerque's North Valley. Walker purchased the stock of an Oklahoma nursery that was going out of business, moved some of the plants to Treeland, and planted rows of junipers (*Juniperus* spp.) and other evergreens east of La Quinta to screen the residence. Ruth Simms, Rose Greely, and John Gaw Meem had originally kept the view to the east across open fields, to the distant Sandia Mountains. By the 1940s there was an extensive orchard, visible on MRGCD plat maps as a grid of regularly spaced trees, which over time lost the regular spacing as trees died out. Walker created a shaded woodland garden with meandering gravel paths and sitting places under a dense canopy of trees for his wife, Victoria. The garden was preserved and integrated into later expansions. According to the Los Poblanos District National Register of Historic Places inventory nomination form, the Walkers made two improvements to the La Quinta gardens. They replaced a chain-link fence that closed in the pool with a wall that matched the original walls seamlessly and that distanced the entrance drive farther east of the pool.

In addition to valley cottonwoods (*Populus deltoides* spp. *wislizeni*) and golden raintree (*Koelreuteria paniculata*), repeated from other places at Los Poblanos, two outstanding trees from the woodland garden continue to thrive. Umbrella pine (*Pinus densiflora* var. *Umbraculifera*) is an upright-growing, flat-topped conifer with bright green needles and beautiful rusty red bark, a dominant tree in the woodland part of the garden. The Kentucky coffee tree (*Gymnocladus dioicus*) has dark green compound leaflets on very long mid-ribs that give it a stark appearance when it defoliates in autumn. White, lightly scented flowers and thick brown seedpods containing beautiful dime-size dark brown seeds, which were roasted and ground to make a coffee substitute by early settlers, are part of the thread of history so integral to Los Poblanos.

Jesus Dominguez began working for Walker in 1979; his influence in the gardens has been continuous since then. He remembers planting the London plane trees (*Platanus* × *acerifolia*), the ponderosa pines (*Pinus ponderosa*), and the rows of junipers east of La Quinta from the Treeland Nursery stock in 1980, as well as composing the woodland garden from the nursery inventory. The woodland garden was first called the Japanese garden because of the umbrella pines (*Pinus densiflora* var. *Umbraculifera*) and other conifers that Dominguez pruned as specimens. The pines are still a vital part of that garden, but a dense shrub understory that includes beauty bush (*Kolkwitzia amabilis*), with clusters of pink flowers in spring and papery shredding bark exposed to view in winter; narrow-leafed boxwood (*Buxus* spp.) edging some of the paths; and years of self-sown raintree, mulberry, and other woody volunteers would completely obscure the earlier design if not

Jesus Dominguez, veteran farmer, lavender distiller, and musician. Jesus has been a mainstay of the gardens of Los Poblanos for forty-two years. His norteña band, Los Paisanos de Chihuahua, occasionally entertains at Campo. Photograph by Carlos Alejandro.

A boxwood maze remnant was preserved during the first phase of garden expansion. The maze was an homage to the Rose Greely Garden, created by Robert Walker during his tenure as steward of the landscape of La Quinta. Photograph by the author.

for the strong networks of pathways that meander the space. Periwinkles, both *Vinca major* and *Vinca minor*, and English ivy (*Hedera helix*) are the primary groundcovers still in evidence, with pockets of Lenten rose (*Helleborus orientalis*) for unexpected blooms very early in the year. Although planted with mostly exotic species, this garden space has been called the "wild garden" and enjoyed by visitors for more than forty years.

In contrast, immediately east of La Quinta, between the rows of nursery stock conifers and La Quinta, Walker also had Dominguez plant a boxwood (*Buxus microphylla* var. *Japonica*) parterre, or maze, that evokes Greely's beaux arts formality. He installed a large fountain, centered on the Grand Portal, on the lower terrace. The fountain was dismantled long ago, but a portion of the parterre has been preserved, honoring the evolution of designers and plant lovers who have contributed to the gardens through the decades. To the north of the fountain area was another series of garden rooms, the centerpiece of which was a planting of sheared blue junipers (*Juniperus chinesis* spp.). No sign of that planting remains, but Dominguez was quick to lead me to the spot and described the large

Scot's pine. Pinus sylvestris is another remnant of the Walker planting at La Quinta. Adapted to difficult climates and soils, Scot's pine, also known as European red pine and Baltic pine, continues to thrive in the gardens and along Rio Grande Boulevard. Photograph by the author.

his crew. They were sheltered in an area that was planted as a pine forest until they recovered and could be returned to Treeland. This area served as a further privacy buffer from Rio Grande Boulevard and was partly cleared of fifty-four pines for the new guest parking area for La Quinta. A few Scot's pines (*Pinus sylvestris*), with their distinctive flaky, copper-colored bark, remain as part of the continuing story of the gardens. During the Walkers' tenure at La Quinta, Dominguez had many roles, from acequia irrigator to landscape gardener, courier, and chauffeur. His role grew to include lavender farmer and distilling assistant for the Rembes.

La Quinta Again Joins Los Poblanos

By late in the 1990s, the children of both the Rembe and Walker families had gone on from Los Poblanos to attend universities and pursue their adult lives. Victoria and Robert Walker moved to Ireland, and the La Quinta property was once again in danger of being subdivided for development. In 1999 newly retired Penny and Armin Rembe purchased La Quinta from the Walkers, and Los Poblanos was granted special use zoning by the village of Los Ranchos to operate as a six-room bed-and-breakfast. The hacienda became Los Poblanos Inn, and La Quinta was restored to public use as a cultural center for small meetings, retreats, and social gatherings. To preserve the character of the village, the entitlement allowed very limited daytime events at the repurposed La Quinta. From 2000 to 2005, the Rembes were the consummate innkeepers. Their attention to detail in providing a welcoming home away from home for guests was paramount, but it soon became apparent that more needed to be done to secure the future of Los Poblanos.

rectangular hedge—head high with an open center and only one entry point, a hidden sitting space within the garden. As the caretaker, he kept all the hedges neatly manicured.

Farther east of the rows of junipers and the wild garden was a sorting and recovery area for Treeland Nursery plants. Large, boxed specimens that were damaged and unsaleable were brought to La Quinta to be rehabilitated by Dominguez and

Beginning Farm and Garden Collaborations

Penny Rembe emphasizes, "It was very important to the Simms that Los Poblanos agricultural lands be preserved," and that continued to be a goal of the Rembes. A step in that direction was placing the fourteen acres along Rio Grande Boulevard in a community land trust, which preserves the land solely for agricultural use in perpetuity. The fields that had been family vegetable gardens became a proving ground for innovative local agricultural models as Erda Gardens and Los Poblanos Organic Farm, two community supported agriculture (CSA) projects, grew in the space. The commitment to educating the next generation continued as several young farmers there grew in their understanding of regenerative farming before they moved on to pilot their own programs.

Sister Marie Nord and Erda Gardens

Sister Marie Nord was a Franciscan nun. Her ministry included growing healthful produce in a way that restores life to local farmland and builds community around food. She founded Erda Gardens and Learning Center in 1996 as the core of her ministry, teaching adults and children sustainable farming. Between 1998 and 2001, eight thousand pounds of salad greens, onions, herbs, tomatoes, beans, peas, and turnips were organically grown on an acre of land at Los Poblanos. Nord's ministry was inspired by San Ysidro. She said, "This is about protecting the earth, restoring one little corner of the planet, and providing food for people." She died suddenly in 2001, but Erda Gardens continued and her ideas became part of the land ethic at Los Poblanos. With new leadership, Erda Gardens moved to the South Valley soon after. Monte Skarsgard quickly filled the role of farmer at Los Poblanos.

San Ysidro. The patron saint of farmers has become a recognizable figure in the story of the gardens of Los Poblanos. This carving done by a local chainsaw artisan holds the hoe used for decades by Los Poblanos's prime acequia irrigator, Carmen Lucero. Photograph by the author.

The San Ysidro Celebration

Even before moving to Los Poblanos, the Rembes had been interested in retablos and santos, a natural extension of their passion for New Mexico history, art, and architecture. Retablos are religious iconography and altarpieces dating back to medieval times. In New Mexico, retablos are Spanish folk art pieces. Some are historic, but many are contemporary, created by renowned artisans. Santos are similar religious images representing saints, usually having special significance and beneficial influence over human lives and livelihoods. San Ysidro is the patron saint of farmers, gardeners, and laborers tied to the land. One of the most common stories about this saint's devotion is that he was a poor but hardworking farm laborer, and while he knelt in prayer, angels tilled his fields. The Peter Hurd mural on the east wall of the Grand Portal at La Quinta illustrates this tale, and the door handles into the building recall elegant plowshares to honor the saint. A John Gaw Meem–designed tile on a wall at La Quinta depicts San Ysidro and his oxen standing in front of La Quinta, indelibly linking the saint to Los Poblanos. There is also a life–size wood carving of San Ysidro on the north side of the lotus pond, and he is represented on the labeling of lavender and most other Los Poblanos products. His feast day is celebrated on May 15, with an alfresco lunch shared by the staff and family at Los Poblanos since 2007, when Father Tom Steele—Jesuit scholar, historian, collector of santos and retablos, renaissance man, and friend of many local farmers—gave the first blessing.

Monte Skarsgard and Los Poblanos Organics CSA

Monte Skarsgard grew up a few miles from Los Poblanos, playing in the fields of the North Valley, and wanted to follow his family's century-old farming tradition. Continuing their commitment to local agriculture, in 2003 the Rembe family leased three acres of farmland at Los Poblanos Inn to Skarsgard to develop a CSA. In the CSA model, people in the community buy shares in future production to give farmers working capital, better crop prices, and a guaranteed market. In return, investors receive a dependable supply of locally grown produce. Seventeen customers and a commitment to growing organic produce were the small beginning of what has become Skarsgard Farms. After nine years, having outgrown the three-acre space, which had been expanded to twelve acres at Los Poblanos, Skarsgard broadened his business to market as many locally grown fruit, vegetable, egg, meat, and milk products as local farmers could supply to now are more than three thousand loyal CSA members. With the Rembes' encouragement, Los Poblanos Organics became Skarsgard Farms and moved to thirty-five acres with twelve thousand square feet of greenhouse space in the historic Los Padillas neighborhood in the South Valley. The Rembes are happy to have shared the Los Poblanos name with such an outstanding farming business and are proud of the many young farmers who spent time training here before going on to their own farming enterprises in the Rio Grande Valley and beyond.

Lavender Fields, Lavender Salve, Lavender Festivals

The genesis of what has become the major crop and the basis for many of the body care products created at Los Poblanos was the planting of three hundred 'Grosso' and 'Provence' lavandin, two cultivars of *Lavandula × intermedia*, by Armin Rembe and Jesus Dominguez in the spring of 1999. The plants were set out in the native clay soil in raised rows to provide better drainage in a sunny, acequia-irrigated field. The following spring, three hundred each of 'Grosso' and 'Provence' were planted in soil deeply amended with compost and fine gravel to further improve drainage. That autumn, five hundred cuttings of each variety were potted and overwintered in the greenhouse, along with several varieties of English lavender (*Lavandula angustifolia*) for planting in May 2002. The Rembes were looking for a pest-resistant crop that could be grown with limited water and that could exceed the value of the water and land it took to produce it. They found that crop in lavender.

Penny Rembe, Sue Brawley, and Susan Keith teamed up to survey their neighbors about their priorities for the village of Los Ranchos. This was a skilled collaboration of community-minded women with business, agricultural, and organizing experience. Brawley was a volunteer comanager of the Los Ranchos Growers Market. Keith was serving on the Middle Rio Grande Council of Government's Agribusiness Task Force. According to Rembe, their survey found that "the most important thing to residents was preserving the agricultural land that was all getting sold off and built on. So we tried to figure out how to save the land, how old people could stay on their land and grow something the whole village could join in on—and the model was the Sequim Lavender Festival."

Sequim, a small farming community on the Olympic Peninsula in Washington State, was losing its agricultural base to development when, in 1995, a small group of neighbors sought to curb the loss of good farmland to suburbanization. They looked for a high-value, low-water crop. On its website, the Sequim Lavender Festival boasts, "Great ideas, like well-acclimated plants, take root easily." Los Ranchos had the added advantage of much more sunshine. In 2004 a Lavender Day celebration was the small beginning of what became a major event,

and the Lavender in the Valley Festival was born. Within five years, nearly twenty thousand people were attending. The gardens and farm of Los Poblanos played a substantial role in the Lavender in the Valley Festival and served as a local resource for neighbors who wanted to join in the lavender growing trend, since by 2004 lavender had been growing at Los Poblanos for several years.

'Grosso' and 'Provence' *Lavandula × intermedia* are hybrids of *Lavandula angustifolia*, commonly called English lavender, and Portuguese or spike lavender (*Lavandula latifolia*). Lavandins are much higher in camphor content than *Lavandula angustifolia*, and that is likely what gives them greater disease resistance and greater healing value. The camphor content in the essential oil of *Lavandula × intermedia* is 6% to 10%, while the camphor content of *L. angustifolia* is less than 0.6%. *Lavandula angustifolia* and varieties such as 'Hidcote' and 'Sharon Roberts' have a sweet floral scent and are best used in cooking and to flavor drinks and ice cream. *Lavandula × intermedia* varieties have a resiny herbal scent and are used for body care products, including therapeutic salves. 'Grosso' lavender retains its flower spikes as it dries, making it a good choice for decorative uses, while 'Provence' tends to shatter easily, a quality that expedites stripping the stems to fill sachets.

Lavenders are native on rocky slopes in Portugal, Spain, southern France, and Italy; lavender is also commercially grown in the foothills of the Balkan Mountains in Bulgaria. France and Bulgaria are currently Europe's major producers. The climate and alkalinity of soil and water at Los Poblanos are excellent for lavender production, but drip irrigation has replaced acequia flooding, both because flooding tends to undermine the sharp drainage that lavender needs and because twenty-first-century Rio Grande water contains

Lavender harvest. The lavender season became a major event at Los Poblanos as more plants produced an abundant harvest. Photograph by Wes Brittenham.

Lavender growing has been an ongoing learning experience at Los Poblanos. Early on it became apparent that the plants preferred better drainage than the acequia-irrigated fields provided. Here Armin and Matt Rembe assess the depth of trenches in a new field, where clay soil would be replaced with a well-drained mix. Courtesy of Los Poblanos.

unfiltered pharmaceuticals that preclude labeling acequia-irrigated crops as organically grown.

As the lavender fields expanded to meet demand, local interest in lavender also grew. Armin Rembe became an ambassador for lavender, encouraging his neighbors to cultivate the well-adapted shrub and sharing lessons being learned at Los Poblanos. Looking for value-added products to support Los Poblanos's lavender production, Penny Rembe began producing lavender salve in small batches in her kitchen. The lavender salve, as healing as it is wonderfully aromatic, became the anchor of the Los Poblanos product line. Armin began to distill lavender oil and hydrosol with help from Jesus Dominguez and later Jamie Lord. For a small fee, guests could cut their own lavender in the fields, a popular hands-on activity.

At the Lavender in the Valley Festival, a gazebo was set up for tea, and the menu featured ham and watercress tea sandwiches, salmon and dill on pumpernickel, and lavender lemon curd tartlets. The first vendors at the festival included Cleofia Martinez with herbs and Beth Crowder, of Sparrow Hawk Farm, with honey. Participating vendors soon expanded to include Fourth Street merchants who sought exposure to many more Albuquerque residents than advertising alone could offer. Park-and-ride shuttles became a necessity as lavender, locally grown foods, and local crafts all became accessible to a very receptive market.

As small local farms and local artisans came to be known and celebrated, the festival grew and more activities were needed, including ways to entertain the young children attending. The fanciful mention of fairy wings in a conversation triggered an idea. Perhaps being the grandmother of small children aided in the leap from fairy wings to a fairy garden, but Penny thought of the wild garden, with its deep shade and winding pathways,

Drying lavender. Part of the original greenhouse is used for drying cut lavender that is not immediately distilled. Photograph by Wes Brittenham.

Lavender in the Village Festival. At the festival and in the neighborhood at large, the Rembes became ambassadors for lavender, encouraging their neighbors to cultivate the well-adapted shrub and sharing lessons learned at Los Poblanos. Photograph by Wes Brittenham.

a perfect setting for "fairy houses" nestled in the greenery. So the festival added tours of the "fairy garden" for the youngest visitors. Their wide-eyed searches for resident sprites are likely childhood memories that still bring smiles to now grown-up faces.

By 2004 Los Poblanos was fostering more than lavender. Its reputation as both an inn and a cultural center was gaining ground, and change always arouses unease. The neighbors were divided in opinion. Some appealed the special use zoning decision in district court, fearing that increased commercial development of the historic property would undermine the quality of life for surround-

ing residents. Other neighbors cited the Rembes' ongoing commitment to historic preservation in the community in support of a family enterprise that would be both financially viable and maintain the cultural values of Los Ranchos. A settlement in 2007 disallowed Los Poblanos from obtaining a beer and wine license, continued to limit the number and size of events, and prohibited the hosting of large weddings.

Matt Rembe returned home to Los Poblanos from New York City in 2004 with a BA in Spanish, an MBA from the Thunderbird School of Global Management, and a decade of work experience as director of Mary-Anne Martin/Fine Art in New York City, where he specialized in twentieth-century Latin American masters. As his childhood experiences at Los Poblanos had foreshadowed

Three generations of the Rembe family, many of whom have served as Los Poblanos board members. They are the minds and hearts behind the evolution and preservation of this special place. Photograph by Sergio Salvador.

his career path, so his education and work experience were great preparation for his next venture. He organized the Los Poblanos board of directors—his parents, siblings, and extended family members—to put together a master plan for the future of their existing businesses: the restaurant, lavender production, lodging, and farm shop—all small with the potential to grow. Matt also brought with him a valuable partner in life and work, Teresa Easton Rembe, who balanced his energy and skills with her refined palate and deep knowledge of food. Matt credits Teresa as the inspiration for the emphasis on regenerative farming and local foods.

This family of strong and accomplished individuals is united by querencia, the love of Los Poblanos and New Mexico, and that made Matt's ambitious vision for preservation and managed growth possible. As executive director of Los Poblanos, he observes, "To create the purest paradigm for historic preservation directing residential and public uses remains our mission." Reliance on market-driven solutions to achieve the preservation goal is still very much in the air and water at Los Poblanos. Matt brought the family a host of questions about Los Poblanos's strengths and where they intended to go with them: How to manage growth? How to learn about travel cycles, and how does that fit with agritourism and preservation? Should they look for outside advisers? What bankers would they need? How to best use social networking, advertise, develop a brand strategy, and develop a budget? How to connect and communicate with their neighbors? What are the Rembes' core values? How to incentivize a growing management team?

Jay Rembe, board chairman, says that the basis for their decision-making was to keep the family invested together in the future of Los Poblanos, not only as a valuable asset but as the core of who they are as a family. He is proud of how his brother has grown as a leader. Penny Rembe concurs: "Matt is the reason we were able to keep up with the changes, innovate, hire, set up systems, hire and keep staff, keep his board (the family) happy, and work with the community." Matt Rembe describes it as working to stay true to the mission.

Sources, and an Invitation to Dig Deeper

Carlos Alejandro Photography, https://caphoto.com.

Dominguez, Jesus. Conversations with author, 2021.

Lavender in the Village Festival, http://lavenderinthevillage.org.

Rembe, Jay. Conversations with author, 2021.

Rembe, Matt. Conversations with author, 2007–2021.

Rembe, Penny. Conversations with author, 2020–2021.

Rembe Urban Design + Development. "Jay Rembe, CEO and Founder." Rembe Urban Design + Development, 2022, https://www.rembedesign.com/the-company/jay-rembe.

Rio Grande Agricultural Land Trust, https://rgalt.org.

Scott, Damon. "Los Poblanos Organics Now Skarsgard Farms." *Albuquerque Business First*, February 21, 2012, https://www.bizjournals.com/albuquerque/news/2012/02/21/los-poblanos-organics-now-skarsgard.html.

Simms, Mary Field. Personal correspondence with author, 2021.

University of New Mexico Medical Center Library Oral History Project. "Interview with Albert G. Simms II, MD." New Mexico Digital Collections, 1984, https://nmdigital.unm.edu/digital/collection/nmhhc/id/188/.

CHAPTER 5

A New Preservation Model: Living History, 2005-2014

Before it can ever be a repose for the senses, the landscape is the work of the mind. Its scenery is built up as much from strata of memory as from layers of rock.

—Simon Schama, historian

The years 2005 to 2007 simmered with collaborative consultations on business programming, preservation modeling, and balancing the pros and cons of various changes as a means of conserving history while sustaining Los Poblanos confidently into the future. A defined mission gained momentum. The Rembes consulted with Susan Henderson, architect, strategic planner, and principal at PlaceMakers, an experienced town planner, urbanist, adviser, and advocate for livable land use and preservation of historic properties. The discussions helped clarify the Rembes' preservation vision and refined the relationship between intended activities and the current mission in order to ensure financial viability while realizing the intended outcomes of any changes made to the estate. One of Henderson's great contributions was her facility for engaging with the village of Los Ranchos to gain the entitlements needed to achieve the mission. She was impressed with the level of engagement of Rembe family members in critiquing proposals from the perspective of their particular expertise. A vision and goals coalesced: "Our mission is to preserve the historic Los Poblanos Ranch by cultivating a dynamic business dedicated to regenerative agriculture, hospitality, historic preservation, and community." After much discussion and many drafts, Matt Rembe, executive director of Los Poblanos Inn and Cultural Center, submitted a detailed proposal to the Los Ranchos board of trustees. The proposal included the hosting of weddings, a greater number of events, beer and wine service at farm-to-table culinary events, and slightly longer hours of operation.

The proposal included letters of support from Nancy Meem Worth, daughter of John Gaw Meem; George Pearl, an esteemed New Mexico architect and Meem scholar; James Moore, then director of the Albuquerque Museum; Richard

Peck, then president of the University of New Mexico; and Mark Childs, an architect, a professor at the University of New Mexico School of Architecture and Planning, and a Los Ranchos resident. Katrina McCormick Barnes, daughter of Ruth Simms, wrote, "I would like to impress upon you the joy that I felt in seeing what you are doing in and around her [Ruth Simms's] last effort in life. She would approve of every step. I approve of every step and deeply appreciate your imaginative toils to this end." To further reassure the neighbors, the proposal highlighted the history of Los Poblanos, cited the thirty years of careful stewardship the Rembes had already demonstrated, and outlined in detail the constraints the family was willing to impose on themselves, emphasizing, "The nature of a successful experience at Los Poblanos hinges on the serenity and tranquility of the property." Querencia, the strength of character needed to grow a future firmly rooted in tradition and remaining true to the mission, was shown to be a strength of the Rembe family.

Finally, in 2008, on-site planning began with Stefanos Polyzoides of Moule & Polyzoides, Architects and Urbanists, on a first-phase expansion of the inn and cultural center. Matt Rembe credits Polyzoides with impressing upon him the importance of landscape architecture in the evolution of Los Poblanos. Having grown up surrounded by the beauty and complexity of the landscape, Rembe took the garden setting for granted. A statement Polyzoides made remains fixed in Matt's memory of early discussions. "Farmers are the best landscape architects." That is, they know and respect the site, soils, and microclimates and what they can provide when attended carefully. "Our family's decades on the property, watching thousands of sunsets, storms, and seasons pass, gave us a unique collective knowledge and wisdom that made us

good clients and collaborators" was Matt's assessment of his family's role in the process.

An accomplished architect, Polyzoides was also a cofounder of the Congress for the New Urbanism and is currently a professor and dean of the School of Architecture at the University of Notre Dame. He proposed a three-part strategy that began with the land itself. Placing more than half of the property in a permanent agricultural trust would protect it from suburban encroachment. The original Meem structures were adroitly adapted to support the country inn concept, and additional inn accommodations were designed in a utilitarian style that referenced the simple and functional 1930s dairy barn and milk house of the Simms era. Essential to the character of Los Poblanos, Polyzoides's design included a variety of courtyard spaces that were also reflective of the historic landscape.

Polyzoides highly recommended Dennis McGlade of Olin Studio in Philadelphia as the landscape architect for the project. After touring Los Poblanos on Google Earth, McGlade, who is known for his international expertise in adaptive reuse—revitalizing historic landscapes to modern-day relevance—visited the site. He was enlisted to design the landscape master plan, with the goal of blending the new landscape with the historic gardens coherently and sustainably. McGlade's deep understanding of the relevance of history in the spirit of a place and his global experience of the opportunities and constraints of specific site conditions made his engagement in the project a perfect alignment of stars. The landscape would continue to serve present and future needs while celebrating its past.

The first phase of expansion was in part to accommodate increased requests for hosting events, especially weddings. Architecturally, the program

Moule & Polyzoides's rendering of the addition to the hacienda on the left and new Meem–inspired suites on the right. The drawing shows the relationship between historic buildings and new spaces under the canopies of the original valley cottonwoods. Graphic provided by Moule & Polyzoides.

Moule & Polyzoides's rendering of the Farm Suites shows new architecture surrounded by historic features: the pond in the foreground to the right, the silos farther right, and the barn as the backdrop. While the Meem Suites are easily recognized as linked in style to historic architecture, the contemporary Farm Suites deftly incorporate 1930s dairy building style, a leap forward for Los Poblanos but with great respect for the past. Graphic provided by Moule & Polyzoides.

was to remodel several existing Meem outbuildings as guest rooms and add architecturally similar suites of rooms around an interior garden space adjacent to the historic inn. *La merienda*, the light meals offered at the bed-and-breakfast, evolved into a fine-dining venue at the inn; executive chef Jonathan Perno took the reins of the restaurant. The dining space expanded. A sun porch breakfast room and a covered patio on the northwest corner of the inn offered a sunrise view of the Sandia Mountains across the lotus pond and extended dining into the gardens. The chef's local-sourcing farm-to-table philosophy blended seamlessly with the Rembe family land preservation ethic and Teresa Rembe's refined palate. The gardens through the seasons, family farmers as a community, and menus built on culture merged as Rio Grande Valley cuisine. Farm-to-table banquets held in La Quinta became much anticipated food-centered social events. The ghost of Ruth Simms was smiling.

Matt Rembe–orchestrated planning charettes for the expansion included the family, the architects, the landscape team (sometimes including the gardeners), and occasionally the inn and kitchen staff, housekeeping, and essentially anyone who would be negotiating the paths with arms full and focused on tasks while doing their best to make the guest experience seamless. The different perspectives of all the parties involved would minimize future glitches, facilitate communication across territorial lines, and spur new ideas that would make life a bit easier for everyone.

Garden Programming

In the gardens, new and renovated guest rooms would have individual patio spaces enclosed with walls, fence panels, or shrub plantings. Paving would be pervious to allow plant roots access to the water and air needed to keep them robust. In the Southwest, *agua es vida*—water is life—and roots are the trees' conduits of precious water as well as their anchors in the wind. Gardens that thrive across time are those that cater to the soil and the roots in it. Main pathways would be hard-paved, while paths for casual exploration of the grounds would be crushed stone or shredded wood, depending on the adjacent planting. Part of the plant selection process was integrating plants from the historic garden areas that continued to be vital and were likely to remain so into the future to create a continuum from the oldest spaces to the newest plantings. Ultimately, plants were selected for resilience, with more heat- and arid-adapted species, better suited to the warming, drying climate, blended into the palette.

Larger gathering spaces were designed as open-air invitations for guests to enjoy the gardens. From the Meem and Greely Suites and the restaurant, shady portales and the scent of roses and herbs would lure guests into the gardens. McGlade used the "hide and reveal" strategy for drawing people into the landscape. Hide and reveal is a design concept drawn from early Chinese paintings, filtered through the lens of the English Romantic garden design tradition of William Robinson, and applied to American landscapes by Frederick Law Olmsted. It creates depth by revealing only part of the story of the space illustrated, which is an open invitation to explore the garden further. In the gardens of Los Poblanos, the prospect of discovery leads visitors through Simms-era garden rooms into newly repurposed spaces for the Meem Suites that are subtly canted in response to the historic meander of the adjacent acequia. A functional aspect of the communal spaces and pathways flowing in and out of each other is maintaining airflow through the gardens, essential for comfort in the hot summertime.

Farm Suites plaza water trough. The central patio visited by songbirds and pollinators, a cat named Mouse, and the occasional peacock all might urge guests to explore the gardens. Photograph by the author.

The Farm Suites' central patio, with a trough water feature visited by the official Los Poblanos greeter, a personable cat named Mouse, and the occasional preening peacock, might lure guests to explore the gardens. The common-area portales draped with banksia roses (*Rosa Banksiae*) and hops (*Humulus lupinus* var. *neomexicanus*) and the small private sitting areas shielded by pomegranates (*Punica granatum*), rosemary (*Salvia Rosmarinus*), and a fig or two (*Ficus carica*) provide places to relax in the shade or bask in the sun. As in Rose Greely's time, objectives for the expansion included plantings for shade, for screening, and as a wear-resistant groundcover and the aesthetic considerations of seasonal color, a balance of evergreen and deciduous plants, and plants with complementary shapes and leaf densities to fit various spaces. Los Poblanos has always been a place where the long view prevails, and the payoff has been a beautiful, functional landscape across more than ninety years. The expansion of the gardens was an exercise in learning from the past and planning for the future. According to Dennis McGlade, "The new aesthetic might be found in the issue of regeneration and sustainability."

While construction was underway, the lavender

festival hosted at Los Poblanos moved across the boulevard to the newly established Los Ranchos Agricultural Center and Open Space. Los Ranchos is one of only few small communities with a dedicated village farmer on staff. Fergus Whitney, who had managed the farm at Los Poblanos, moved across the boulevard to take on that position. Lavender was blossoming in Los Ranchos, a village-wide program directed by community members. The mission of the Lavender in the Village Festival is to "preserve and enhance Los Ranchos public open space, stimulate an interest in sustainable agriculture, with an emphasis on educating the public, including such matters as historic agriculture, lavender, and its uses, and fostering community spirit." Los Poblanos Inn and Organic Farm is a living, evolving model of that mission.

Los Poblanos Inn Garden Adaptation and Conservation

I begin this tour of landscape transitions with a well-loved and preserved space. Like an aging beauty with elegant bone structure, the Rose Greely Garden was not significantly changed in form and only slightly altered in content during and since the first phase of expansion. Most significantly from a water conservation perspective, while the garden might occasionally be flooded to maintain a connection to the acequia system, drip irrigation was installed to keep the plants in their prime while reducing the amount of water used. Several renovated rooms open onto the original wisteria (*W. sinensis*) arbor. Dripping with purple blooms in spring and cool in summer, this front porch offers a long view of the Greely Garden. The original borders of golden raintree (*Koelreuteria paniculata*), burkwood viburnums (*V. × burkwoodii*),

western cane (*Arundo donax*), black locust (*Robinia pseudoacacia*), Lady Banks roses (*Rosa banksia* 'Alba' and 'Lutea'), and deeply rooted peonies (*Paonia* spp.) were left undisturbed. No need to challenge successes.

Roses have always been an integral part of the plant palette at Los Poblanos. Even prior to the Simms era, native *Rosa woodsii* grew along the Rio Grande, likely for thousands of years. Its roots knit the soil together, preventing erosion; its pink blossoms in spring provide both pollen and nectar for bees and butterflies; and its red rosehips in summer and fall are foraged by birds and harvested by herbalists. Over the years, some of the original rose selections were replaced. Others were declining in the Greely Garden beds, and apothecary cultivars, to be used in distillation, were planted. In addition to the distillation of lavender oil, Los Poblanos Organic Farm distills other flower and herb essences. Distilling rose oil and rose water requires roses with intoxicating fragrances—the apothecary varieties. The array of gorgeous colors is a bonus for distillation and the joy of the garden.

Traditional roses used for distillation include *Rosa gallica officinalis*, one of the first cultivated rose species, native across southern Europe and Turkey into the Caucasus; *Rosa damascena*, called damask rose in the Middle East and rose of Castille in Spain; *Rosa centifolia*, called cabbage roses because of their densely packed petals; and a relative newcomer introduced in 1886, Bourbon rose, a hybrid of *Rosa gallica* and *Rosa chinensis*. Damask rose is itself a hybrid of *Rosa gallica*, *Rosa moschata* musk rose, and *Rosa fedtschenkoana*. These species and hybrids offer a range of wonderful scents— some fruity, some spicy—and colors in a range of pinks, reds, whites, and yellows. Their flower forms range from single with predominant centers

Roses have always been an integral part of the plant palette at Los Poblanos. Penny Rembe chose 125 David Austin roses for replanting in the Greely Garden. These cultivars with improved disease resistance are rich in color and the fragrances needed to make hydrosols. Photograph by Wes Brittenham.

Pistache autumn color in Greely Garden. A Chinese pistache (*Pistacia chinensis*) was added to the west terrace of the inn to buffer the blazing summer sun and provide brilliant autumn color. The pistache roots deeply and will not undermine paving, critical in preserving the 1930s pebble mosaics. Photograph by Wes Brittenham.

of golden stamens to semi-double to fully double with densely clustered petals. They typically have one bloom period, from mid-spring into summer, are disease resistant, and are adapted to soils relatively low in organic matter, a common condition in arid regions.

Penny Rembe chose one hundred and twenty-five David Austin roses for the Greely Garden.

David C. H. Austin was a highly respected English rose breeder, teacher, and author who crossbred the heritage roses—the gallicas, damasks, and albas—with modern tea and floribunda roses to create varieties that have the grace, fragrance, and resilience of the old roses but that also bloom repeatedly in an even wider range of colors and flower forms. From the first introduc-

Ficus carica is becoming even better suited to the Rio Grande Valley as the climate warms. Its abundant fruit is a versatile menu option. The bold branch structure, large leaves, and aroma are ornamental assets. Photograph by the author.

tion, 'Constance Spry' in 1961, Austin produced a prodigious array of "modern heirlooms" and set a standard for excellence in rose cultivars during his more than fifty-year career. After more than a decade in the Greely Garden, the vibrant color display and the fruity, spicy, and sometimes citrusy scents of the Austin roses continue to delight visitors.

Another minor change in the Greely Garden was adding a Chinese pistache (*Pistacia chinensis*) to the west terrace of the inn to buffer the blazing summer sun. One of few truly heat-and-drought tolerant mid-size trees, pistache has been increasingly used for shade in arid landscapes since the 1990s and has been widely adopted in Albuquerque as the urban heat island effect has compounded climate change in the Southwest. Until at least a dozen years old, young pistache trees have all the grace of a hat rack, but they root deeply and do not undermine paving. Pop Shaffer's pebble mosaic tributes to Ruth Simms's prized livestock Judge and Grumpy are close by, and deep roots that would not in time crumble Grumpy were necessary.

The following recipes used at Campo feature fruit produced in the gardens.

Blue Cheese–Stuffed Figs

INGREDIENTS

8 figs, washed
2-ounce piece of blue cheese
4 slices prosciutto

PREPARATION

1. Trim the stems off the figs. Cut each fig in half. Crumble the blue cheese and place a few pieces of cheese into each section of fig.
2. Cut each slice of prosciutto in half and place them on a baking sheet lined with parchment or wax paper. Bake for 5–8 minutes at 350 degrees or until crispy. Remove the prosciutto and place it on a platter. Lay one piece of fig on each piece of prosciutto.
Serves 4
  Recipe courtesy of Los Poblanos archives

Wild Rice, Sweet Red Pepper, and Pomegranate Seed Dressing

INGREDIENTS

1 cup wild rice
2 whole garlic cloves
1 large bay leaf
1 teaspoon salt
4 cups water
4 roasted and peeled sweet red peppers, diced
2 cups extra virgin olive oil
1 cup Spanish sherry vinegar
Salt and pepper to taste
Pinch of sugar
1 bunch of parsley, chopped
2 cups pomegranate seeds

Punica granatum flowers, and fruit. Even if the juicy, tart, jewel-like seeds aren't your favorite, the pomegranate is a gem of an ornamental garden shrub, with brilliant vermillion blossoms and sculptural fruit. Unharvested fruit eventually splits open to reveal the seeds, which are quickly harvested by songbirds, who recognize a good thing when they find it. Photograph by the author.

PREPARATION

1. In a 2-quart sauce pot, add the water, rice, garlic, bay leaf, and salt. Bring to a boil and then turn heat to low and simmer until rice is tender. More water may be added as necessary. Drain the rice once it is cooked and remove the bay leaf and garlic cloves. Set the rice aside.
2. Mix the vinegar, salt, pepper, and sugar together in a large bowl. Whisk in the olive oil and then fold in the rice, peppers, pomegranate seeds, and parsley.
3. Adjust the seasoning with salt and pepper.
Serves 6
  Recipe courtesy of Los Poblanos archives

Figs (*Ficus carica*) and pomegranates (*Punica granatum*) were added to the Greely Garden in earlier generations. The fig tree may have been cutting-grown from figs at the Alvarado Hotel, a historic Harvey House in downtown Albuquerque that was demolished in the early 1970s. Pomegranates were added by the Rembes soon after they arrived. Both are Mediterranean natives, and while they tolerate our ultimate high and low temperatures, rapid changes can cause problems. The fig tree in the Greely Garden has frozen back to half its size several times in the past fifty years. After remedial pruning in late spring, it recovered to bear fruit abundantly later the same year. Pomegranates seem to be less troubled by sudden deep freezes. Overall, growth and fruit production are affected more by access to water while blooming and fruit is developing. Both figs and pomegranates were planted in the new gardens. As the climate warms, they are becoming even better adapted to growing conditions and a modest water budget and are a great source of fruit for the Los Poblanos kitchens.

North of the Greely Garden, new Meem-inspired territorial revival–style rooms were added. They enclose a small lawn and a new valley cottonwood (*Populus deltoides* spp. *wislizeni*), planted to replace an original cottonwood removed to build one wing of the addition. A purple leaf plum tree (*Prunus cerastifera*) and a scholar tree (*Styphnolobium* syn. *Sophora japonicum*), one of the Simms-era tree selections, were added for shade and seasonal color. The pink flowers of the plum are harbingers of spring, and if there are no deep frosts after it blooms, small burgundy red plums develop. The plums are delicious and infuse drinks and preserves with a deep claret hue. The clusters of small white blossoms of the scholar tree scent the air and hum with bees in summer, when many flowering plants take a siesta in the heat. Pomegranates (*Punica gra-*

natum) were added in the wider borders to repeat the pomegranates the Rembes had added in the Greely Garden years before, and a Bourbon climbing rose (*Rosa* 'Zephirine Drouhin') was planted on the south side of the rooms, where it can be seen from the sunroom, greet passersby with its scent, and extend the apothecary rose collection into this adjoining living space.

A raised planter immediately north of the Greely Garden gate was built on top of a former parking area west of the inn's new sunroom and was dedicated to herbs for the kitchen only a few steps away. These include French tarragon (*Artemisia dracunculus* 'Sativa'), bronze fennel (*Foeniculum vulgare* 'Dulce'), 'Arp' rosemary, (*Salvia Rosmarinus*), culinary sage (*Salvia officinalis*), English thyme (*Thymus vulgaris*), culinary oregano (*Origanum* spp.), licorice mint (*Agastache rupestris*), and chives (*Allium schoenoprasm*). Bush mint (*Zizophora clinopodiodes*), spearmint (*Mentha spicata*), lemon balm (*Melissa officinalis*), and Greek germander (*Teucrium majoricum*) were added as groundcovers in the surrounding shrub beds. Aside from their culinary value, these plants were selected for a balance of evergreen foliage in winter, their nectar-rich pollinator blooms, and their delicate aromas wafting on the cool morning and evening air. After the second expansion, when kitchen activity shifted to the new Campo restaurant, many of these herbs were relocated to beds closer to that hive of activity. Pollinator-attracting perennials and wildflowers were planted in their place.

Farm-inspired spaces, the Barn Commons and Farm Suites, were built across the north acequia from the Meem renovation, where the original family vegetable and cutting gardens had been. A venerable weeping mulberry tree (*Morus alba* 'Pendula') was carefully excavated with a large tree spade, transported to the prepared site with a crane, and replanted near the west side of the old milking barn and silos, where it joined an existing weeping mulberry. Both continue to thrive, yielding delicious fruit for the kitchen every summer. The draping branch canopies create hobbit-like hiding places for young guests under their tents of down-curved branches. The Barn Commons, a meeting space, gym, and outdoor saltwater pool, and the Barn Suites, guest rooms in an adaptive reuse interpretation of 1930s Department of Agriculture vernacular dairy buildings with pitched tin roofs, white stucco walls, and a rustic grape arbor, signal the transition from preservation of the historic garden feeling to modern-adapted planting.

Western chokecherries *Prunus* (*virginiana* spp. *melanocarpa*), pomegranates (*Punica granatum*), figs (*Ficus carica*), rosemary (*Salvia Rosmarinus*), jujubes (*Zizyphus jujuba*), and yerba mansa (*Anemopsis californica*), a traditional medicinal plant native to the nearby bosque as well as a beautiful garden groundcover in the shade, share space with Lady Banks roses (*Rosa banksia* 'Alba' and 'Lutea'), wisteria (*W. sinensis*), and 'Coronation Gold' yarrow (*Achillea fillipendulina*), plants adopted from the historic plant palette. Soft-leafed yucca (*Y. recurvifolia*) was planted where pathways pass near guest room windows as the yuccas are massive enough to screen the windows, but their flexible leaves are not a danger to passersby or window washers. This native of coastal dunes in the southeastern United States adapts well to much less annual rainfall and slightly saline soil conditions and has a deeper green leaf color when grown in the shade. It blooms with candelabras of waxy white flowers, similar to the southwestern desert species, but it typically blooms in both spring and fall while the desert natives have a single flowering period in summer. At Los Poblanos, soft-leafed

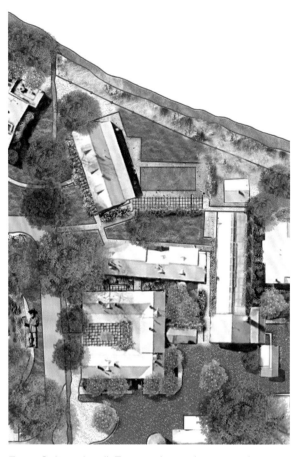

Farm Suites detail. Farm-oriented spaces, the Barn Commons and Farm Suites, were built across the north acequia from the Meem addition in 1930s USDA dairy farm vernacular style. Pitched tin roofs, white stucco walls, and a rustic grape arbor signal the transition from historic preservation to modern adaptation. The north acequia flows from the Griegos Lateral at the top of the drawing along the south side of the Barn Suites. The historic greenhouse is on the right. Jujube trees wrap the southern edge (bottom of detail) of the suites. Graphic by Hannah Aulick and the author.

Farm Suites and silos. The design concept for the first expansion was to make the transition from the historic gardens to modern use as seamless as possible. Many plants thriving in the established gardens for half a century were integrated into the plant palette with more heat-loving, drought-tolerant options. The density of planting remains lush as shown in this image of the Farm Suites across the drive from the lotus pond. Photograph by the author.

yuccas also signal a transition from wetter-climate exotics to arid-adapted natives.

Coral honeysuckle (*Lonicera sempervirens* 'Magnifica'), a southeastern native with hummingbird-attracting clusters of orange flowers, was added to drape the heirloom garden edging. It was a last-minute solution when, near the end of the first phase of construction, HVAC units sprouted like mushrooms after rain. Thanks to the quick thinking of Matt Rembe, heavy twisted

wire fencing that had been stored for decades in the old dairy barn was rolled out to support the honeysuckle, planted to screen the units. Vines are usually fast growing and can reduce the brash newness of construction, so English ivy (*Hedera helix*), Boston ivy (*Parthenocissus tricuspidata*), woodbine (*Parthenocissus vitacea*), the locally native species of Virginia creeper, wisteria (*W. sinensis*), and Lady Banks roses (*Rosa banksia* 'Alba' and 'Lutea') were woven into the plant palette from the historic plant

Farm Suites patios. Each suite has a small patio tucked between plantings. Soft–leafed yucca, pomegranate, rosemary, and yarrow suggest enclosure. Heavy twisted–wire garden fencing that had been stored in the old barn for decades was resurrected to screen the very contemporary HVAC units. This photo was taken in the autumn of 2013. The planting has since filled in to provide green walls between the suites. Photograph by the author.

selection. In wetter climates, vines can become difficult to manage as they sprawl and creep across a garden, but our scarcity of moisture is an asset in curbing vine enthusiasm. Carolina jessamine (*Gelsemium sempervirens*) is used on some suite fence enclosures because it is easy to manage as a green wall, with the added benefit of lightly fragrant yellow flowers in early spring. Cultivars of table grapes (*Vitis vinifera*) and New Mexico hops (*Humulus lupulus* var. *Neomexicanus*) were added to the edible palette.

The Farm Suites have niche patios screened from each other with figs (*Ficus carica*), pomegranates (*Punica granatum*), rosemary (*Salvia rosmarinus*), and chokecherries (*Prunus virginiana* var. *melanocarpa*). Some patios have wood plank walls with wisteria (*W. sinensis*) woven between the planks. One of my favorite hidden spaces in the gardens is the persimmon courtyard. It is enclosed on three sides by casita walls and on the north side separated from the historic greenhouse by an evergreen privet (*Ligustrum*) hedge that is a fragment of the original Simms cutting and vegetable garden screen. Paved with flagstones, this space is shaded

One of my favorite hidden spaces in the gardens is the persimmon courtyard, shown here just two years after it was planted. Keystone plants are three 'Fuyugaki' persimmon trees (*Diospyros kaki*), elegant small trees with crisp glossy leaves and plump salmon-colored fruits. The fruits hang like jewels from bare branches until harvested in autumn. Photograph by the author.

Persimmon fruit. Photograph by the author.

by a canopy of three 'Fuyugaki' persimmon trees (*Diospyros kaki*). Persimmons are elegant small trees with crisp glossy leaves. Their plump salmon-colored fruits hang like jewels from the trees' bare branches in autumn, until the pastry chef determines that the non-astringent fruits are perfect for harvesting.

Los Poblanos Persimmon Morning Glory Muffins

INGREDIENTS

2 cups all-purpose flour
1 ¼ cups granulated sugar
2 teaspoons baking soda
2 teaspoons cinnamon
¼ teaspoon salt
2 cups Fuyu persimmons, diced small
1 apple, cored, peeled, and shredded
½ cup raisins
½ cup unsweetened coconut flakes
3 eggs, lightly beaten
1 cup vegetable oil
2 teaspoons vanilla syrup

PREPARATION

1. Preheat the oven to 350 degrees F and grease and flour muffin tins or line with paper cups.
2. In a large mixing bowl, combine flour, sugar, baking soda, cinnamon, and salt.
3. Stir in the persimmons, apple, raisins, coconut, and pecans.
4. In a separate bowl, mix the wet ingredients. Gently fold the wet mix into the dry mix until just combined.

5. Scoop batter into the muffin tins and bake for 20 to 30 minutes.

Makes 18 muffins

Recipe courtesy of Los Poblanos archives

The La Quinta Garden Evolution

The new gardens surrounding La Quinta were designed to blend with the historic garden in form and planting as much as possible. Directly east of the Grand Portal and historic tiled swimming pool, the grade drops to a lower terrace that in Ruth Simms's day was the edge of cultivation, where farm fields and pasture were the foregrounds to a sweeping view of desert grassland east to the Sandia foothills. This vista was later framed by Ponderosa pines (*Pinus ponderosa*) and London plane trees (*Platanus × acerifolia*). At some point early on, pasture grass and an apple orchard were planted. The remaining evidence is the gnarled trunk and delicious fruit of a venerable heirloom tree bordering the present-day vegetable gardens and new orchard. In the Walker era, the space was planted with rows of junipers as a privacy screen.

The repurposed decorative iron fence and gates with the AR (Albert and Ruth) brand bisect wide beds above and below a retaining wall, with a gracious wide brick stairway connecting the levels to the wedding garden lawn. The landing was intended to serve as a stage for wedding ceremonies, the lawn as a greensward reception space. The beds are asymmetrically balanced in their planting with 'White Cascade' and 'Prairie Fire' crabapples (*Malus domestica*) cultivars, white Meidiland groundcover roses, 'RainbowKnockout' roses (*Rosa* cultivars), compact and creeping mahonia (*M. aquifolium* 'Compacta' and *M. repens*), white and pale pink peo-

nies, 'Husker Red' penstemon (*P. digilalis*), gaura (*Oenothera lindheimeri*), and other perennials.

The rows of junipers planted in the 1970s were removed to create the ceremonial lawn, but the sycamores (*Platanus × acerifolia*) and pines (*Pinus ponderosa* and *Pinus sylvestris*) that framed the mountain view for decades were preserved, as was a portion of the boxwood parterre, the maze from Walker's time, and the wild garden—the magical overgrown space with paths looping through overhanging trees and flowering shrubs that Robert Walker planted for his wife, Victoria. 'Cecile Brunner' climbing roses arch over trellises that separate a smaller outdoor gathering space from the main wedding garden lawn.

Low stone retaining walls and an ornamental ironwork fence separate the upper La Quinta terrace from the lower lawn area. A wide flight of formal brick-paved platform stairs flanked by flower and shrub beds was added to lead from one level to the other and provide a stage for ceremonies and elegant photo opportunities. The beds are planted with 'White Cascade' and 'Prairiefire' crabapples (*Malus domestica* cultivars), 'Rainbo Knockout' roses and white Meidiland roses (*Rosa* hybrids), 'Grosso' lavender (*Lavandula × intermedia*), 'Husker's red' penstemon (*P. digitalis*), dwarf plumbago (*Ceratostigma plumbaginoides*), compact mahonia (*M. aquifolium* 'Compacta'), and creeping mahonia (*M. repens*). These more contemporary plant choices were selected because they have greater disease and insect resistance than some of the earlier planting. Burkwood viburnum (*V. × burkwoodii*) and peonies (*Paonia*) are stalwarts borrowed from Simms- and Walker-era plantings to add flower power and seasonal interest.

The new landscape worked around the existing pines and plane trees, but multiple rows of junipers were removed to open the space for the lawn and a double row of lacebark elms (*Ulmus parvi-*

Ceremonial garden at La Quinta. The garden was developed during the first expansion phase to accommodate weddings and other large ceremonies. The more recently developed elm hybrid 'Allee' was chosen to reference the historic elm allée. The newer selection of elm is more pest–resistant and will be somewhat smaller at maturity. La Quinta is seen in the background. Photograph by the author.

folia 'Emer II') to shade it. McGlade's master plan took flood irrigation of the existing large trees into account, and it is telling that the established shade trees and conifers didn't suffer in the renovation. While turfgrass is rightly maligned for its excessive water use in the desert, no practical living ground-cover alternative is as wear-resistant year-round. Ongoing turfgrass research is aimed at producing more heat- and drought-adapted cool-season lawn grass, but endophyte-enhanced fescue sod is still the preferred green cover in heavily used areas. Endophytes are beneficial microorganisms that infiltrate the roots of the host plant and, growing outward,

extend the plants' ability to absorb water and mineral salts needed for growth. Endophyte-enhanced fescues are more resilient than fescues that are not inoculated. Paved surfaces, although more wear-resistant than turf, absorb and reradiate heat too effectively for comfort and are a major component in the urban heat island phenomenon that is rapidly making southwestern cities less comfortable. At La Quinta, the plan was to use sprinklers to establish the lawn but to use the acequia to flood-irrigate the lawn and trees intermittently, as was done for generations.

Flood irrigation is sometimes rejected as waste-

Acequia irrigation of the hacienda lawn. The lawns south of the hacienda (shown here) and north of La Quinta continue to be flood–irrigated from the middle acequia. Flood irrigation keeps the mature trees healthy and helps establish extensive roots on newly planted trees. Photograph by the author.

ful, and it is true that cool-season lawns require more than four times the local precipitation than falls in a good year. When a field is laser-leveled, so that irrigation water moves relatively uniformly across the surface and quickly soaks into the soil, and the soil is amended with compost to retain water more effectively and improve water-holding capacity, excess water from flood irrigation can infiltrate to deeper tree roots and ultimately percolate to the shallow aquifer and help maintain continuity with the river across the basin. Sprinkler irrigation has a high cost in evaporative loss, even with spray heads engineered for efficiency and watering

carried out during the coolest part of the day to minimize evaporation. Groundwater is mined to supply sprinklers, which depletes the shallow aquifer, so it is generally the least conservative way to irrigate. Compared with the value of shade trees in cooling the air and providing layers of wildlife habitat, lawns are a costly amenity that is best reserved for the most heavily used public and play spaces.

As flows in the Rio have decreased due to less snowmelt and as warmer temperatures have increased evaporation rates from open water and at the same time increased transpiration rates, the MRGCD has implemented many conservation measures to assure that irrigation water remains available for farming, traditionally considered the highest and best use. Recent initiatives include repairing and rebuilding control structures, rehabilitating conservancy canals to prevent leakage and provide precise, measured delivery, monitoring the shared use of water diligently, and timing access to acequia water at a rate of one acre per hour. To support small farmers' efforts to irrigate efficiently, farms of less than ten acres are prioritized for educational, technical, and financial assistance when funding is available. Combined, these actions are all means of making less water go further to produce more food locally. The goals are to keep small farms productive and to maintain the connectivity of the shallow aquifer to the river. Currently, Los Poblanos only flood-irrigates once a month, supplemented with drip irrigation of food and other organic crops without jeopardizing the gardens, evidence that careful planning and water conservation efforts are working.

Acequias are a tradition with deep roots in the Rio Grande Valley, and they were the sole water source for these lands for generations. The shallow water table recharged with acequia water that filters through the soil has maintained the cottonwoods. At Los Poblanos, since historic preservation is a major consideration, the desire is to maintain as much acequia use as is practical. Unfortunately, the soil saturation that allows for less frequent and deeper irrigation with flooding became a disaster for events using the lawn areas. The saturated soil dries slowly, a plus for water retention but a soggy mess for guests at an event. The compromise became sprinklers irrigating the few most heavily used lawns and flooding of the historic tree and shrub plantings as well as the less heavily used lawns north of La Quinta and south of the inn. Low-flow and drip irrigation is used for most of the crops and the new gardens planted in shrubs and perennials,

all part of the paradigm of adaptive historic preservation meeting present-day constraints.

The wedding garden lawn is shaded with 'Allée' elms (*Ulmus chinensis* syn. *parvifolia Emer II*), a trademarked selection of lacebark elm, arching in parallel rows, a reference to the historic Siberian elm and cottonwood allée that continues to be the main approach to the property. The tall arching branches of the elms are cathedral-like in presence, reinforcing the ceremonial intention of the space. The long east–west axis of the ceremonial garden ends in a massive territorial-style wall with brick detail, repeating the architecture of La Quinta and the adjacent Walker-era wall, softened with Boston ivy (*Parthenocissus tricuspidata*) and English ivy (*Hedera helix*). 'Skyrocket' junipers (*Juniperus scopulorum*), a slender upright form of native Rocky Mountain juniper, and white crape myrtles (*Lagerstroemia indica*) bookend the view, with 'Double Pink Knockout' and 'Ballerina' roses (*Rosa* hybrids) and 'Grosso' lavender (*Lavandula × intermedia*) as fillers between the taller shrubs. The wall separates this serene space from a graveled parking area and screens the view of suburban housing that has replaced the Simms-era view of farm fields, but it underlines the view of the Sandia Mountains from the Grand Portal of La Quinta. The parking spaces are arranged between rows of Russian hawthorn (*Crataegus ambigua*), the most heat- and drought-tolerant hawthorn species, and 'Radiant' crabapples (*Malus domestica* cultivar). These resilient trees buffer the gravel paving and harken back to the apple orchard that once grew there.

The choice of tree species to grace the wedding space, which was designated as ceremonial and therefore layered with meaning, was personally instructive and illustrates the often messy collaborative process, sometimes likened to sausage making. Brainstorming sessions usually involved six or more people: always Matt Rembe, Dennis McGlade and his team from Olin Studio, and I; almost always Penny, Armin, and Jay Rembe, with input from the chefs, the farmers, and housekeeping when their feedback was needed. At first, crabapples were proposed as an option for the shade canopy of the wedding garden. We talked about varieties that would grow large enough to have visual impact and yield the necessary shade canopy, varieties with subdued color to complement any bridal color scheme, and varieties with small fruit and enough persistence to minimize maintenance. Finally, Dennis suggested what in retrospect was obvious: that we think about the prospective bride who is dazzled by the floral display when visiting and then schedules her wedding for the same weekend a year later.

While crabapples are consistent in creating an intense flower show, there can be a two-week or longer spread in bloom time, influenced by a cold winter, a slow spring warm-up, or a warm winter and perhaps an early bloom. So when a bride arrives for one of the most significant days of her life, already a bundle of frayed nerves, she might find the crabapples in tight bud or the flowers blown, with petals littering the sod. It's best to avoid an emotional catastrophe. After more discussion, we decided on the cathedral-like arching branches and soothing green foliage of a variety of lacebark elm (*Ulmus chinensis* syn. *parvifolia*), which also relates to the history of the gardens.

McGlade observed that "Of all the elements that make up a designed landscape, I think plants elicit some of the most basic, universal responses, responses that in many ways are quite ageless. For instance, our discussions about how to grow things, our frustrations, and our successes. Pliny the Elder, a Roman scholar from the first century, wrote about his kitchen and flower gardens, as well as the trouble he had with figs . . . People's perceptions and reactions don't change. I think someone in ancient Rome would react the same way to being

in a beautiful garden on a spring day with the birds singing and the air fragrant with blossoms as you or I might." This sentiment is the heart of the gardens of Los Poblanos, inviting guests to experience the power of plants.

Not every choice was as pivotal, and often there were several alternatives, but I have imagined Rose Greely and Ruth Simms weighing their options with equal care and without the aid of video conferencing. It was a joy to select plants for gardens where 'Black Satin' blackberries (*Rubus ursinus*) could be considered as an edible hedge where a barrier to foot traffic was needed, where rhubarb (*Rheum × hybridum*) might be used in a shady rainwater basin as a bold-leafed ornamental as well as a source of juicy stalks for cobblers and tarts, and where cardoons (*Cynara cardunculus*) might be accepted as a stunning architectural perennial that could also serve the kitchen. Los Poblanos is a place where plants matter.

In 2013, the National Trust for Historic Preservation lauded the work at Los Poblanos Inn and Organic Farm with its Trustees Emeritus Award for Excellence in the Stewardship of Historic Sites. The trust recognized the value inherent in Los Poblanos's market-driven preservation paradigm—inviting gentle use of the property to generate the funds to preserve it rather than attempting to freeze it in time. For the gardens in particular, this is a wise strategy, as climate change increasingly limits the viability of exotics from wetter, cooler climates. Having a historic preservation designation in no way guarantees that a property will be protected from deteriorating beyond repair. Continuous stewardship and the financial wherewithal to perform needed maintenance can be an onerous undertaking if there is not a viable plan and the foresight to adapt. A market-driven plan that generates an appreciation for the history, art, and culture that makes a place valued, and the funding to preserve, it is often the

La Quinta royal raindrops crabapple. Crabapples were included in the new planting to frame the view from the Grand Portal. They are part of the transitional plant palette, borrowing from the historic gardens in places where existing plants require more frequent but shallower irrigation. Their brilliant display of fruit provides color from late summer well into winter, when the sweetly fermented fruit attracts songbirds for a cocktail. Photograph by the author.

best scenario. "Los Poblanos is a true gem for the community and for visitors from across the globe," said Stephanie Meeks, president of the National Trust for Historic Preservation. "Its natural beauty and comfort—combined with its fascinating history and character—make it one of the most magnificent historic properties in the Southwest."

The New Paradigm

In 2011, with the first phase of construction complete, it was time to grow into the changes, to live the new business plan. It is a blueprint for supporting people, place, and planet and for making a profit to meet future demands. The overarching goal is to systematically activate the entire twenty-five acres while preserving the culture embodied in the architecture and landscape. The plan maintains the fourteen acres along Rio Grande Boulevard as preserved in perpetuity for agriculture, an essential part of the culture of Los Poblanos and the middle Rio Grande Valley. The gardens continue to be a hybrid of carefully selected exotic ornamentals and edible plants, with native plants to maintain a link to the origins of this very special place. Lavender remains the signature crop, with potential for value well beyond that of the resources

Matt Rembe and Jonathan Perno at the Lavender Festival, a community event supported by Los Poblanos. Classes on various topics related to growing and processing lavender and samples of lavender cuisine are well-received. Here Matt emcees while Jonathan tends to the food. Photograph by Wes Brittenham.

Armin Rembe distillation demo at the 2013 Lavender Festival. Armin Rembe gave distillation demonstrations at the Lavender in the Village Festivals to promote the value-added crop to visitors and neighbors interested in the process. Courtesy of Los Poblanos.

needed to grow it, but the cultivation of personal relationships with fellow farmers, plant lovers, neighbors, and guests is the true regenerative harvest.

Sources, and an Invitation to Dig Deeper

Arellano, Juan Esteban. *Enduring Acequias: Wisdom of the Land, Knowledge of the Water.* Albuquerque: University of New Mexico Press, 2014.

Henderson, Susan. Conversation with author, 2021.

Los Poblanos. "Celebrating San Ysidro Day." Los Poblanas, 2022, https://lospoblanos.com/blog/celebrating-san-ysidro-day.

Middle Rio Grande Conservancy District, https://www.mrgcd.com.

Moule & Polyzoides. "Los Poblanos Inn & Organic Farm." Moule & Polyzoides, 2022, https://mparchitects.com/site/projects/los-poblanos-inn-organic-farm.

National Center for Complementary and Integrative Health. "Lavender." NCCIH, November 15, 2022, https://www.nccih.nih.gov/health/lavender.

Olin, https://www.theolinstudio.com.

Olin, Laurie D., Dennis C. McGlade, Robert J. Bedell, Susan K. Weiler, David A. Rubin, and Lucinda R. Sanders. *Olin Placemaking.* New York: Monacelli Press, 2008.

Rembe, Jay. Conversations with author, 2021.

Rembe, Penny. Conversations with author, 2021.

Schama, Simon. *Landscape and Memory.* New York: Alfred A. Knopf, 1995.

A bird's-eye view of the master plan for the gardens of Los Poblanos shows a work in progress. The Griegos Lateral is at the top of the image, Rio Grande Boulevard is at the bottom, north is to the right, and the band of trees south of center, bordering the lavender fields, is the historic elm allée, the main entrance to Los Poblanos.

A garden is never "done." This rendering tells the story of the gardens across time. The brightest green lawns and tree canopies are established spaces and are still supported to some degree by acequia water. They still maintain a direct connection to the Rio Grande. While edible plants are threaded throughout the gardens, the historic architecture and ornamental landscape dominate the top third of the site, following the bend in the Griegos Lateral. These gardens are a series of outdoor rooms that complete the functions of the architecture they adjoin.

Drip-irrigated row crops and fruit trees occupy the east half of the site, with lavender shading the land in silver and purple. Salad greens, herbs, tomatoes, dozens of other seasonal crops, and rows of flowers for cutting stain the land in colorful stripes. Maize and sunflowers buffered by silverberry (Elaeagnus pungens) hedges screen the northwest streetscape.

Guest parking separates the current farm gardens, below the parking lots, from the historic architecture and gardens. The new fingers-in-the-field suites, inn reception area, Campo, Bar Campo, and Farm Shop are north of the lavender fields. The land use blurs human and wildlife habitat, food gardens, and prairie. More than half the land is farmed and will continue to be. The farm fields enrich the guest experience and maintain the sense of peace and well-being that pervades the gardens. Graphic by Hannah Aulick and author.

CHAPTER 6
Focus on the Future, 2015-2020

If conservationists are serious about conservation, they will have to realize that the best conserver of the land in use will always be the small owner or operator . . . who knows how to use the land in the best way, and who can afford to do so.
—Wendell Berry, agricultural ecologist

The next chapter of the story seems to fast-forward into a new future. Penny Rembe started making lavender salve in her kitchen as a remedy for gardening-chafed hands, a small batch at a time, adding value to the crop grown. Twenty or more years later, salve was still being produced in small batches, in a slightly larger kitchen, by a team of "worker bees," but the salve was now the anchor of the Los Poblanos Organic Farm lavender product line and marketed internationally. An upgrade in production facilities was in order. At the same time, preservation of the historic buildings meant increasing the number of new inn rooms to reduce daily wear on historic spaces. Updating facilities involved repurposing, rebuilding, and expanding the old milk barns to add more manufacturing and retail space and transitioning the restaurant from the old inn to Campo.

As the inn has grown, Los Poblanos executive director Matt Rembe, an advocate of all things New Mexican, and Los Poblanos executive chef Jonathan Perno, a farmer, butcher, and locavore, have built relationships with many small farmers in the Rio Grande watershed and beyond, as well as with La Montañita Co-op, to source staples not viably grown in New Mexico. The Los Poblanos farmers focus on what they can grow best on-site and experiment with crops the kitchen would like to work with or that complement the produce of the other partner farmers. In this way, Rio Grande Valley cuisine is the creative result of what the land best yields, with food built directly on local culture. Credit is given to the people who grow the crops, as well as to chefs who transform local produce into gourmet meals. A challenge of playing close to home with ingredients nourished by the Rio Grande is that you have to expect surprises, improvise, and change. The Rembe family, Los Poblanos farmers, and Campo chefs associate a lasting change in the way food is

Christopher Bethoney, head chef, harvests mul–
berries for the evening's appetizers at Bar Campo.
Photograph by the author.

Field to fork. An hour later, a goat cheese, mul
berry, and spring onions tartlet graces the plate of
an appreciative diner. Photograph by the author.

raised with elevating consumer expectations. As people experience fresh local food served seasonally at the height of ripeness, the expectation of what should be available at local markets and offered in local restaurants changes for the better. The way to raise consciousness is to offer high quality consistently. Campo takes what the farmer started to a sublimely palatable crescendo.

Today several synergistic businesses are entwined at Los Poblanos: lodging, farming, food preparation and restaurant service, wholesale manufacturing of lavender and other products, brick-and-mortar and online sales of those products, and hosting of events. The farming is interwoven with the ornamental gardens seamlessly, as herbs, fruit-bearing trees, shrubs, and cardoons (*Cynara cardunculus*) are part of both. Inn and Campo guests are immersed in the gardens, from views to fragrances to drinks and dishes. But ultimately, each business is market-based and accountable for its own profit or loss. Pre-pandemic there were 250 employees; within eighteen months, the team returned to pre-pandemic numbers. Matt Rembe

is the maestro of them all. The vision is his, but he is quick to credit his family and his team of managers and staff for many of the ideas and programs that have added depth to the guest experience and diversified the body care products, food, and drink offered. He credits his wife, Teresa, with focusing on food as a key part of what makes contemporary Los Poblanos successful. How food is raised on the farm and on those of farmer partners, the link between food and emotional and physical well-being—these embody a drumbeat that both Teresa Rembe and the Campo chefs move to.

The team in turn credits Matt Rembe for being open to new proposals and willing to take risks to add value. The Slovenian bee house is an example of the evolution of an idea. Armin Rembe began beekeeping at Los Poblanos soon after the Rembe family moved to the farm. After experimenting a bit, he came to prefer top bar hives, which are easier to manage and more productive than other types. The fact that top bar hives are the oldest and globally the most commonly used hives also appealed to him as a cultural preservationist.

Top Bar versus Langstroth Hives

Top bar hives have trough-shaped boxes that sit up on legs, with individual wooden bars laid across the open hive. Bees build combs down from the bars, without the added wax foundations found in standard box hives. The Langstroth hive, introduced by nineteenth-century American apiarist L. L. Langstroth, is another popular design. In these hives, wooden super boxes measuring 14 by 20 by 6.5 inches contain eight or ten wood-framed inserts coated with beeswax, where bees build their honey-filled combs. Extracting honey from a full super box (weighing forty or fifty pounds) requires lifting it off the hive, pulling out the frames, and usually using a centrifugal extractor to separate the honey from the comb. In contrast, top bars weigh about five pounds and drip honey that is easily separated from the wax. Not only does this type of hive save the beekeeper's back, but it also disturbs the bees much less.

Top bar hives next to the lavender fields. Armin Rembe preferred top bar beehives. Photograph by Wes Brittenham.

The Slovenian bee house in winter, when bees and fields are dormant and sandhill cranes are guests in the safe haven of the gardens of Los Poblanos. Photograph by the author.

In the Slovenian bee house, bees live in cabinet-like enclosures with only two chambers: the brood chamber and the honey chamber. The honey frames slide out of the back of the hive horizontally, and the chambers can be inspected individually by removing an internal screen door. Slovenian bee houses are also called AZ hives, after Anton Znidersic, a Slovenian apiarist and inventor of the late 1800s. He designed the structure to protect bees from severe weather, provide a pleasant space for beekeepers to work, and be easily moved to food sources where bees were needed for pollination. All this appealed to Los Poblanos beekeeper Lara Lovell and director of horticulture Wes Brittenham. Wes went a step further, "thinking inside the box." He finds the hum of bees soothing and thought that once the AZ hive was established, the space could also be used for meditation or even massage with lavender honey body products, with the bees busily producing more just behind the screens. While none of this has begun, the bee house is large enough to someday accommodate it.

Beekeeping in the gardens at Los Poblanos is an example of how the different businesses are integrated and reciprocally interdependent. Bees pollinate the food crops, increasing productivity and supplying the Campo restaurant kitchen with fresh produce. Via Campo chefs, the Farm Shop is supplied with tempting preserves. Conversely, the abundance of nectar-rich blooming plants assures a long season of nourishment for bees; the exotic plants support honeybees, which are themselves exotics, and the native plants support native bees—potentially hundreds of species.

Adaptive Evolution of Los Poblanos Inn: Fingers in the Fields

As early as 2012, it was apparent that constraints in the entitlement granted by the village of Los Ranchos were at odds with fully realizing the goals of Los Poblanos, so negotiations with the village were reopened to "right-size" the entitlements. The goodwill already built within the community eased the process. The second phase of planning for construction began in 2015 with dinner around Penny and Armin Rembe's farm table. Shawn Evans led the team at Atkin Olshin Schade (AOS), which designed the second expansion renovation. Dennis

McGlade at Olin Studio returned to develop the master plan for the landscape.

Carrying on the design of the 1930s dairy-style buildings introduced in the Farm Suites by Stefanos Polyzoides in the first-phase additions, the new pitched tin roofs and walls alternating between white stucco, stained wood, and corrugated metal are simultaneously modern and traditional. AOS renovated the main farm structures, moved Campo into the remodeled barn complex, and extended it with a new commercial-grade kitchen measuring twenty-eight hundred square feet. The Farm Shop was expanded and moved into the renovated milking barn, with a new lavender production facility added north of the original barns. A new inn reception building and twenty-eight new guest suites were built, extending the inn into the lavender fields.

Evans notes, "The mode of design at Los Poblanos has . . . created a wonderful division between the historic buildings designed by Meem and the more informal, relaxed, and agrarian architecture of the barns, the Farm Suites, and the Field Suites. . . . There's a slow conversation between the historic farm buildings, the Farm Suites, and other Moule & Polyzoides buildings and our work. People read them differently—some seeing the tradition, some seeing the contemporary, some seeing both and the dance between."

The unpretentious agrarian architecture acts in concert with the gardens to allow the historic Meem buildings to remain the focus and to encourage guests to slow down and really experience Los Poblanos. Evans considers the new buildings in the fields as "lovely to look at, but they're really intended to work the other way: to allow views, understanding, and experience of the setting—the sounds of the acequia, the smell of the lavender, focused views on the Sandias—and to

Atkin Olshin Schade overview of Los Poblanos, placing the site in context and highlighting the project expansion. Graphic provided by AOS; drawings prepared by Renee Reder for AOS.

encourage gathering and serendipitous encounters and conversations while also providing privacy without isolation. The various landscapes . . . share the duality of formal and informal, designed and utilitarian, garden and field. For me, the success of this place in both buildings and landscapes is the wonderful balance between luxury and humility."

Garden goals have shifted. They are now focused on what will work best in a hotter, drier future, to bring inn guests and Campo diners into the lavender fields and to surround them with food plants and desert-adapted species that support native bees and honeybees, butterflies, and songbirds. Planting for current and future ecological realities of less water and increasingly hotter and drier growing conditions was a shift away from the exotic species of the Simms era. This phase fully integrated farm into garden and garden into farm, a "fingers in the field" immersive experience. Conservation is not a low-cal diet tolerated for planetary health. It is instead the richest possible feast, the reward for exercising natural curiosity and dedication to place. Babylonstoren, a farm-to-table adaptation of a historic orchard and vineyard in Franschhoek, South Africa, provided inspiration and a bit of assurance that the concepts work.

Rainwater Harvesting, Reducing the Heat Island, Welcoming Diversity

A tour of the new gardens might begin in the parking lot. In this land where the automobile still rules, expanding the inn meant a larger parking lot. The debate began with the choice between shifting west by cutting into the lotus pond or moving east into the lavender field. Although reducing the pond was more complicated, the demand for lavender products and the idea of extending the new Field Suites out into the farm fields were basic to the concept of the guest experience of waking up to the hum of bees and the scent of lavender on a July morning. The pond surround was reworked to accommodate more parking, and no one, including the ducks and geese, has seemed to notice.

Shading the parking lot was a balancing act between adding as many new cottonwood and elm trees as possible to cover as many paved areas as quickly as possible and still maintaining the needed number of parking spaces. The driving lanes that loop around the lot were asphalted to minimize dust and wear, but the parking spaces themselves are pervious gravel to give tree roots access to rainwater and oxygen. The asphalt is crowned so that stormwater drains toward the permeable surfaces, and a deep French drain runs down the center of the parking lot to capture heavy rain and store it underground. Rainwater that is not stored as a res-

French drain rainwater harvesting in the parking lot solves several problems. Rainwater from the paving runs off the surface and is stored below ground, for plants to tap into as needed. Any excess eventually seeps down to the groundwater, filtered through layers of plant roots, soil, and rock. Mexican threadgrass (*Nasella tenuissima*) and mullein (*Verbascum thapsus*) are camp followers that buffer paving. Photograph by the author.

Plan detail of rainwater harvesting in the parking lot. Mature trees shade the parking lot and pavers cover the hidden French drain running midway through the parking spaces. Graphic by Hannah Aulick and author.

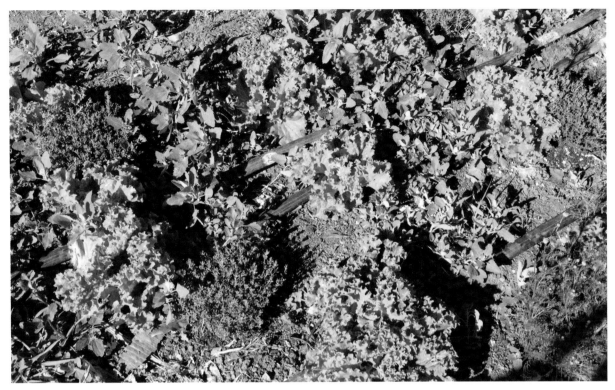

A mixed field of bright green early spring looseleaf lettuce (*Lactuca sativa*) and culinary thyme (Thymus vulgaris) planted alongside the drip tape with quelites (*Chenopodium album*) and chamomile (*Chamaemelum nobile*) volunteers filling gaps in between. These are camp followers, useful plants that take advantage of good growing conditions and are harvested along with the intended crops. Photograph by the author.

ervoir for the roots of the trees shading the parking spaces nearby is cleaned by filtering through layers of soil, recharging the shallow water table. An arbor similar to the one along the south wall of the Barn Commons covers the French drain and the path beneath. Draped with table grapes (*Vitis vinifera*), the shaded pathway runs the length of the parking lot. There, guests can meander in comfort on a blazing summer afternoon and have a lit pathway on moonless nights. The grapes also benefit from the rainwater harvesting reservoir.

Wild annual sunflowers (*Helianthus annuus*) and mullein (*Verbascum thapsus*) have seeded themselves in the tree basins and along the pathway and are left to come and go as they please, as long as they do not block the path or parking spaces. This complicity with the generosity of nature is as common among the gardeners and farmers of Los Poblanos today as it was with the ancestral Tiguex farmers of this land, who diversified their crops with camp followers: edible native plants that self-sowed in places that were amenable. Today many farmers don't recognize the wild greens called *quelites* (*Chenopodium album*) and destroy them as weeds in their sadly monocultural fields. But at Los Poblanos, those tasty and nutritious volunteers, when they are fresh and tender, might make their way into breakfast or lunch at Campo.

Sunflowers as a group are one of the habitat superstores, supporting a host of pollinating insects and then feeding many songbirds into winter. The annual sunflower (*Helianthus annuus*), which bakers often include in loaves of bread and chefs use in mole, is a plant much modified by thousands of years of selection. Puebloan ancestors began selecting the wildflower for larger, thicker hulled seeds or for small, thin-hulled, oil-rich seeds and larger flower heads. The Hopi people selected dark black seeds to use for dyeing fibers. Native to America, sunflowers first appeared in gardens in Spain in the early 1500s.

In Europe, centuries of intensive selection yielded cultivated varieties of *Helianthus annuus*, which became an important crop for oil production. Peter the Great is said to have brought sunflowers to Russia during his travels to western Europe, and Russia now is the biggest producer of sunflowers for both seeds and oil. Russian immigrants to the United States brought the much-changed sunflower back home to America. There are varieties with enormous seed heads, some that grow ten feet tall, and shorter ones with thicker stems that resist blowing over in heavy rains and wind. There are varieties with mahogany, bronze, and red flowers. The farmers at Los Poblanos sow some of the fancy selections for cut flowers or to harvest seeds for the kitchen, but since selections all quickly revert back to the wild form, the prolific sunflowers volunteering in the gardens are natives.

The large, fuzzy, and pale green leaf rosettes and tall cylindrical flower and seed heads of mullein are architectural as well as medicinal. In nature, there is no waste, but in horticulture and agriculture, there is too often unrecognized virtue. A facet of the water conservation ethic at Los Poblanos is to reap as many benefits as possible from the same gallon of water, whether it comes from a well or acequia or is rainwater running off the parking lot. The songbirds feeding on sunflower seeds in winter are complimentary entertainment for human guests. Everything is connected, and diversity is a means of adopting nature's strategy for resilience.

The Gardens and the Farm Fields

From the parking area, there are two main ways to arrive at Campo, the Farm Shop, and the Field Suites. One pathway approaches the inn reception building, framed by low poured-concrete board-formed walls. These rough concrete walls were introduced in the form of low courtyard walls and a bridge crossing the north acequia to the largest Farm Suite courtyard and the trough water feature there. They are repeated as side walls for the bridge across the north acequia to the registration building, as low enclosures for many of the Field Suite patios, as entry walls to Campo, and as the trough water features in all Field Suites courtyards. The impression of the wood used to form the walls is etched in the surface of the walls when the forms are removed, creating a rustic yet modern feel that complements adjacent planting. The beds framing the registration building doorway are bordered with culinary sage (*Salvia officinalis*), 'Mango Salsa' and 'Julia Child' shrub roses (*Rosa* hybrids), and 'Sharon Roberts' and 'Hidcote' lavenders (*Lavandula angustifolia*). These varieties of lavender are sweet and used to flavor drinks and desserts. It is worth mentioning that the 'Julia Child' rose is buttery yellow, with a light citrus-honey fragrance, and is as resilient as its namesake.

The other access to the plaza south of the Farm Stop and Campo, anchored by the iconic Los Poblanos silos, is separated from the parking

A path to the reception building and Field Suites crosses a bridge over the north acequia, framed by low poured-concrete walls etched with the impression of the wood used to form them. The scent of roses and lavender welcomes guests. Photograph by the author.

The wide, less formal path to Campo and the Farm Shop is anchored by iconic silos and framed by jujube trees (*Zizyphus jujuba*), cardoons (*Cynara cardunculus*), and 'Grosso' lavender (*Lavandula x intermedia*), which combine beautifully to blur the line between farm and ornamental gardens. Jujubes are well-adapted to the Rio Grande watershed and valued in many cuisines worldwide. The tree's honey-scented but otherwise inconspicuous flowers and bright glossy leaves take 100°F temperatures in stride. Photograph by the author

area by one of the old London plane trees (*Platanus × acerifolia*) growing along the north acequia. A weeping mulberry (*Morus alba 'Pendula'*) and an old red tractor, a McCormick Farmall retired from service during the Simms era, frame the wide entrance. The plaza between the Farm Suites and inn reception is paved with fine crushed basalt and doubles as an outdoor gathering and dining space. It is bordered with jujube trees (*Zizyphus jujuba*) and sotol or desert spoon (*Dasylirion wheeleri*), cardoon (*Cynara cardunculus*), and hybrid manzanitas (*Arctostaphylos × coloradensis*). A trough

Jujube fruit. Branches laden with bronze–colored oval fruit await the chefs, ready to be added to the seasonal menu. Photograph by the author.

fountain shaded by a Simms-era Siberian elm (*Ulmus pumila*) marks the entrance to Campo. Farther east the space opens onto patios for the bar and restaurant, pétanque courts, and, across the cutting garden and cornfields, a distant view of the Sandia Mountains. There is a strong relationship between the architecture and the outdoor spaces that surround it. The clear mountain views and proximity of farm fields firmly define a sense of place.

Jujube Vinegar

INGREDIENTS

2 cups cider vinegar
3 cups canola oil
1 tablespoon coriander
4 tablespoons orange zest
Pinch of cardamom
1 teaspoon ground ginger
1 ½ cups jujube paste
3 tablespoons Dijon mustard
1 large shallot

JUJUBE PASTE:

2 pounds ripe jujubes (washed and seeded)
4 cups water
2 bay leaves
1 tablspoon salt
¼ cup cider vinegar
2 tablespoons virgin olive oil

PREPARATION

In a 4–quart saucepan, add jujube, water, bay leaves, and salt. Bring mixture to a boil and simmer for 20 minutes. Remove from heat and stir in the oil and vinegar. Place the mixture into a blender in batches. Blend until very smooth. Store in a container; it will last up to two weeks. This mixture can be used to make a vinaigrette or a marinade for meats and fish. It can be added to sauces or used to finish a pasta dish.

Recipe courtesy of Los Poblanos archives

Satisfying Diverse Plant Needs

Mixing fruit trees such as plums (*Prunus* spp.) and crabapples (*Malus* spp.), larger shade trees such as chinkapin oak (*Quercus muhlenbergia*) and scholar tree (*Styphnolobium japonicum*), roses, and other adaptable but less drought-tolerant plants with dryland natives such as 'Pink Parade' hybrid (*Hesperaloe parviflora × funifera*), 'Maverick' honey mesquite (*Prosopis glandulosa*), Arizona rosewood (*Vauquelinia californica*), escarpment live oak (*Quercus fusiformis*), desert willow (*Chilopsis linearis*), fern bush (*Chamaebatieria millefolium*), spineless prickly pear (*Opuntia canacarpa* 'Ellisiana'), and sotol (*Dasylirion wheeleri*) poses challenges. By virtue of their ultimate height and biomass, more deeply rooting shade trees are thirstier than arid-adapted plants.

Chinkapin oak. *Quercus muhlenbergia*, one of the faster-growing heat-adapted regionally native oaks, is used for shade near some farm rooms. Its reddish growing tips in spring and subtle rust-to-burgundy fall colors are ornamental assets, but oaks are also important larval hosts for many butterflies. Photograph by the author.

Escarpment live oak. *Quercus fusiformis*, another fast-growing heat-adapted regionally native oak, is used for shade near some Farm Suites as well as for its evergreen presence in the winter garden. Oaks are also important larval hosts for many butterflies. Photograph by the author.

In addition, desert plants are healthier when they experience dry periods between irrigations. This is a critical issue both when getting new plants established and in meeting the needs of trees rooting as extensively as is necessary for their long-term health.

Not true willows, desert willows (*Chilopsis linearis*) are locally native shrubs that are sculpted as small trees in garden spaces that are too hot and dry for other trees. Their orchid–like flowers attract hummingbirds most of the summer. Photograph by the author.

Sotol or desert spoon (*Dasylirion wheeleri*) is so well adapted that once it's well rooted, it will thrive on rainwater. The strappy blue leaves with toothed margins are evergreen, adding structure to the winter landscape. Its tall spikes of tiny but nectar–rich flowers support dozens of pollinators, and the seeds that follow are food for songbirds. And a ten– to twelve–year–old plant will yield about a liter of the Chihuahuan Desert's smoky–sweet signature liquor. Appropriately enough, sotol can be found just outside Bar Campo. Photograph by the author.

Overall, the succulents and other drought-loving species were planted in hotter, drier niches, so that once established they might be grown on rainfall with little or no supplemental watering. Most desert plants will absorb as much water as they can when the moisture is available, since the next opportunity may be weeks or months away. In the short term, as long as the soil drains well and is not saturated for long, the result is rapid plant growth using the extra water. Soil that stays saturated for longer periods may lack the oxygen that arid land plant roots need, and plants will begin to decline. Wet soil in winter can be deadly for succulents. In addition, the frequent shallow watering needed by most temperate climate plants may stimulate rapid growth, leaving plants that would normally root much deeper to avoid drought more vulnerable to wind breakage and attack by insect pests.

Hydrozoning Irrigation and Building Compatible Plant Communities

Ideally, hydrozoning irrigation—grouping plants with like watering needs and in some cases running parallel water lines (one used more frequently for shorter cycles and the other run for longer cycles much less often)—solves the problem presented by

Hops (*Humulus lupulus var. neomexicanus*) is native along streams in the mountains. Although less consistent in flavor than the European hops cultivars, it is used by skilled local brew masters and grown by savvy gardeners, who use the seedpods dried in bouquets. Photograph by the author.

New Mexico olive (*Forestiera pubescens*) is native along the Rio Grande, blooming in early spring, and is one of the first nectar sources for bees as they emerge from winter dormancy. Small bright green leaves are refreshing in the hot summer sun, and the clusters of blue fruits are a welcome menu item for many songbirds. Photograph by the author.

diverse water needs. The flow rate and number of emitters per plant can also be adjusted to suit individual plant needs. Since cost is a consideration in duplicating water lines for a project as large as Los Poblanos, designers tried to minimize the duplicate lines, transitioning between watering zones by building compatible plant communities. They aimed for a blend of adaptations, with southwestern plants native to wetter niches like the nearby Rio Grande bosque—the native woodland that shadows the river—and natives from higher elevations, which catch more rain and snow than the valley does. Bosque natives that can adapt to more frequent, shallower watering, such as New Mexico olive (*Forestiera pubescens*) and yerba mansa (*Anemopsis californica*), and montane natives such as hops (*Humulus lupulus* var. *neomexicanus*) and golden columbine (*Aquilegia chrysantha*) can be combined with exotics that are flexible in their water demands, such as 'Black Lace' elderberry

(*Sambucus nigra 'Eva'*) and 'Hot Razz' butterfly bush (*Buddleja davidii* hybrid). Other transitional plants selected were cultivars of native plants such as 'Fireworks' goldenrod (*Solidago rugosa*), which is midwestern in origin, and 'Sangria' yarrow (*Achillea millefolium*), which is a less aggressive but more colorful relative of white yarrow that hosts butterflies just as well. These plants tend to respond like typical garden exotics, enjoying a bit more water and some protection from our climatic extremes.

The New Mexico olive (*Forestiera pubescens* var. *neomexicana*) blooms early in spring, before fruit trees such as peaches, cherries, pears, and apples, when bees are just beginning to forage. The olive bears clusters of small blue fruits that songbirds glean as they ripen later in summer and fall. Native in the bosque, where they might be flooded during spring runoff and must root deeply to tap the shallow water table in the Rio Grande floodplain, *Forestiera* adapts to a life of ease with more frequent irrigation. Yerba mansa (*Anemopsis californica*) will become a thick carpet of rubbery green leaves graced with white coneflowers in late spring and summer. It has a fresh aroma that hints at its traditional use as a spring tonic and soothing stomach medicine. After frost in autumn, its leaves turn red and then rusty brown, and they persist as a winter carpet until new leaves emerge in spring. The good news for gardeners is that yerba mansa grows so densely as a groundcover that once it's well developed, it never needs weeding.

Golden columbine (*Aquilegia chrysantha*) is native to higher elevations, which are cooler and receive twice the rainfall of Los Poblanos, but it adapts very well in the valley as long as it is shaded in the afternoon and receives a bit more water. 'Black Lace' elderberry (*Sambucus nigra* 'Eva'), native to Europe, is a large shrub with a filigree of dark purple leaves capped with umbels of pale pink flowers followed by small blue-black fruits. While the flowers and fruit of this variety are not as tasty as those of our native species, the plant seems more resilient to climate extremes, perhaps due to the overall reduced leaf surface and the protective anthocyanins in its foliage, indicated by its deep purple leaf color. Pollinators and birds use both flowers and fruits, so it fits the holistic menu quite well. 'Fireworks' goldenrod (*Solidago rugosa*), a large midwestern perennial wildflower, blooms later in the season and supplies the food that bee and butterfly species that overwinter need to survive, filling another niche in the ecological puzzle that is the gardens of Los Poblanos.

The wooly butterfly bush (*Buddleja marrubifolia*), a Chihuahuan Desert native, is more southern in distribution and is not as cold tolerant as the 'Hot Razz' butterfly bush (*Buddleja davidii* hybrid), a compact cultivar with an extra-long blooming season because it does not produce viable seeds. The deep wine purple fragrant flower spikes of 'Hot Razz' attract bees and butterflies through much of the growing season and make good cut flowers as well. While wooly butterfly bush might work in the hottest, driest spots with minimal irrigation, and after erratically cold winters might require severe pruning, the exotic in this case is more apt to adapt to the transitional irrigation. 'Hot Razz' is used in the garden east of Campo's outdoor dining and firepit patios to provide the animation of pollinators in the foreground without blocking the mountain view beyond. 'Sangria' yarrow (*Achillea millefolium*) and cardoons (*Cynara cardunculus*) are companions as butterfly magnets. The yarrow repeats the butterfly bush color, while the cardoons are a stunning contrast with their clumps of large silver leaves and thistle-like fragrant purple flowers. The thick cardoon stems are harvested for the kitchen. The flowers may be cut for arrangements, left for pollinators and seed harvesting, or distilled in an amaro-like bitter digestif. The original seeding of cardoons was 'Rouge d'Alger,' a North African heirloom variety with purple stems. Seed is collected by the Los Poblanos farmers each year to develop a landrace specifically adapted to local conditions.

A chance encounter with an inn guest one evening illustrates another benefit of cardoons in the landscape. The guest, a visitor from Chicago, was sitting on his patio, intently watching the bees buzzing, landing, sipping nectar, and carrying away pollen from the big purple cardoon flowers. Enjoying the bee dance, he commented that bee watching was as engrossing as birdwatching. We have more than one thousand native bees in New Mexico, plus the honeybees that contribute to the Los Poblanos bakery and Campo—hive to table. The guest was amazed to have observed three different bee species on a single cardoon flower and settled in to add them

Bees on cardoon. While the elegant, incised foliage and large purple flowers of cardoons have ornamental value, they were intended primarily as a crop for the kitchen and have proven to be a great source of pollen and nectar for several species of bees, including honeybees that also supply the kitchen. Bee-watching just outside Field Suite patios has also become a source of relaxed entertainment for guests. Photograph by Wes Brittenham.

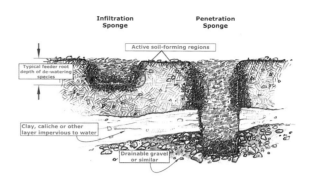

Soil sponge graphic. Courtesy of Jim Brooks and Michael Young, Adaptive Terrain Systems.

to his life list. Small observations add up to deep experience, and for landscape designers, such aha moments in the garden are deeply satisfying.

Soil Sponges

Soil sponges are a soil-building and water-harvesting strategy employed to support fruit trees and shade trees. Subsurface and invisible except for the vigor of the associated trees, soil sponges create in-ground moisture reservoirs and renew soil microorganisms that promote healthy plant growth. They are pits dug at least twelve inches deep and twelve inches in diameter, backfilled with a mix of active compost, shredded wood, and pumice. The compost in the mix increases soil microbial activity to benefit root development, the wood feeds the soil microbes until they colonize the tree roots, and the pumice keeps the mix aerated. This simple, inexpensive technique works much better than the old horticultural approach of amending backfill soil when planting new trees because it restores mycorrhizal organisms, improving soil health without creating a pocket of foreign soil immediately around the roots of a new transplant, which tends to limit root development beyond the amended soil. The native soil then acts as a barrier to root development, rather than benefiting the transplants. Soil sponges reintroduce beneficial microbes to a much larger area as mycorrhizae grow out into the soil spreading out from the sponges. Expanding root systems will tap into the sponges but aren't restricted to them. And tree roots colonized by mycorrhizae have many times the water-absorbing capacity than do uncolonized roots.

Drip Irrigation Benefits and Limitations

Both a great advantage and a drawback, the drip irrigation at Los Poblanos localizes where and how much water is applied to the soil. While this tends to reduce weed invasion by limiting the moisture to only the desirable transplants, to thrive, trees must extend their roots into moist soil beyond their initial planting holes. The larger the tree, the more extensive its root run should be. Soil sponges were installed for all the larger and more moisture-loving trees, including the valley cottonwoods (*Populus deltoides* spp. *wislizeni*), scholar trees (*Styphnolobium japonicum*), chinkapin oaks (*Quercus muhlenbergii*), Texas red oaks (*Quercus buckleyi*), and 'Burkett' and 'Western Schley' or 'Pawnee' pecans (*Carya illinoinensis* varieties). In addition to emitters placed around the perimeters of root balls, emitters are above the sponges to keep the microbes active and to support any roots that infiltrate. In most places, there are drip-irrigated patches of groundcovers to extend areas of moist soil so the trees can root beyond their original root balls. Mexican threadgrass (*Nasella tenuissima*) is planted with the 'Santa Rosa' plums (*Prunus salicina*) and the 'Radiant' crabapples (*Malus domestica* cultivar). Garlic chives (*Allium tuberosum*) are planted with the apricots (*Prunus armeniacum*). These companion plants are less thirsty than the trees they accompany, so much of the water given to them is shared with new tree roots. Imagine the soil microbes and tree roots as an extensive web of life hidden from view but absolutely fundamental to the longevity and vigor of the trees they support.

Semi-dwarf 'Santa Rosa' plums (*Prunus salicina*) and 'Radiant' crabapples (*Malus domestica* cultivar) border the pétanque and cornhole play area, framing views from the bar and restaurant windows and patios. The white-flowered plums are an heirloom variety developed by Luther Burbank in 1906 in Santa Rosa, California, selected for their fruit quality and heat tolerance. The crabapple trees are similar in size and shape, with contrasting deep pink flowers a month or more after the plums bloom. Their persistent small red fruits attract

songbirds in winter, especially as the crabapples begin to ferment and their sugars break down with alternating freezing and thawing temperatures. Designers chose the trees for their culinary uses and for their forms, planted in allée-like rows to refer to the historic entryway planting and the ceremonial garden, but with the added value of fruit for the kitchen. Concern for these trees led to using the soil health–enhancing sponges within their future rooting areas. The shallowly rooted trees are benefiting as the health of the soil is restored by microbial action after being driven over and parked on by construction vehicles, compacting what had been healthy farmland.

Mexican threadgrass (*Nasella tenuissima*) is very xeric, so most of the water applied to this groundcover will go to nearby trees. Other benefits include the cooling green cover of the grasses in summer, their platinum blond color when they are dormant, the graceful rippling of the limber leaf blades in the wind, and the glow of the backlit tassels at sunrise. Several higher-flow-rate drip emitters were placed around the perimeter of the root balls of the trees to start the rooting, and drip lines with emitters imbedded in the tubing were looped through the grasses and over the sponges to encourage the trees to extend their roots across as much area as possible and to keep the microbes in the sponges active. A three-inch-deep layer of shredded wood mulch was added to limit the grass reseeding and insulate the soil. As it breaks down, the wood mulch also feeds the soil microbes that support the trees.

The pétanque courts are paved with a thick layer of basalt fines, which tend to inhibit weed growth. The thick layers of wood mulch and basalt fines quelled nightmares of the threadgrass running amok, as it is known to do, and the graceful gold and green clumps of grass that nod in which-

Mexican threadgrass (*Nasella tenuissima*), backlit by the morning sun, greets guests breakfasting at Campo. The grasses share unseen soil sponges and irrigation water with the obviously healthy plum trees. Photograph by the author.

ever direction the wind is blowing have so far stayed where they are. Grasses are a key component of butterfly habitat; they provide the forage for caterpillars, and caterpillars are the primary food for songbird hatchlings, so the grace, beauty, and water thriftiness of threadgrass are also ecologically valuable. In addition to layers of planting, there are seasonal layers, so beneficial insects and other pollinators and songbirds have something on the menu year-round. They are also guests of the inn.

Ecological landscape design involves layers of thought to develop a balance. Luckily, these resilient plants cooperate readily. Lastly and perhaps most importantly, successfully blending desert native plants with exotic, mostly edible species relies on the nuanced stewardship of dedicated gardeners. This intelligent care is a tradition in the gardens of Los Poblanos, where in the early days, gardeners who had been subsistence farmers tended the exotics first planted in the Simms era. Rose Greely was remarkably astute in her plant selection, especially considering her lack of experience in arid climates, but ultimately the success of the gardens lies in the hands of caretakers who were adept at reading plant response and reacting appropriately. Today we are hampered by our cultural distancing from observation and interaction with plants in nature and in cultivation. Training is required of those who are curious and willing to learn. These are the present-day gardeners of Los Poblanos, people who need their time outdoors with the plants as much as the plants need their care. Many of the artisan farmers in the Rio Grande watershed learned farming skills in these fields, first with the Simms and then with the Rembes. Currently a crew of willing hands is being taught to watch and learn by Wes Brittenham, who has spent much of his career in horticulture, opening eyes and minds to the joys of tending plants.

Garden Design Negotiations

Because the area east of Campo and between two rows of the Field Suites is visible and intended to be well used year-round, there was a great deal of brainstorming involved in piecing together a multiuse plan for the space. Early in 2017, planting options cropped up like tumbleweeds after the monsoon. At first, in keeping with the idea of having the lavender fields come up into the garden, five rows of lavender extending up to the walkway east of Campo were proposed, but that idea was tossed out as perhaps not attractive enough in winter, after harvest and as plants decline and need replacing. Keeping with the row crop, fingers-in-the-fields concept, multiple rows of an ornamental grass separating the pétanque courts were proposed, but since only stubble would remain once routine yearly maintenance was done, designers continued to seek a better solution.

Finally, three rows of long, narrow raised beds of weathered steel gained ground as the best option. Raised beds would keep pétanque players and their boules out of the planting. The rusted steel would strongly define the beds year-round. Succulents and culinary herbs were a good match for the hot growing conditions. They would provide interesting color, texture, and fragrance, and the herbs would be just a quick dash away from the kitchen. The plant mix includes a new compact selection of *Hesperaloe parviflora*, called 'Brakelights' for its brilliant red flowers on two-foot-tall stems, a draw for hummingbirds through the summer; 'Arp' rosemary (*Salvia Rosmarinus*), because it is both heat tolerant and cold hardy and its roots would be exposed to winter cold in the raised beds; culinary sage (*Salvia officinalis*) and garden thyme (*Thymus vulgaris*); 'Ava's' hummingbird mint (*Agastache cana*), a tall, intensely colorful selection with sweetly aromatic foliage and deep rose-purple flowers that also lure hummingbirds; and bronze fennel (*Foeniculum vulgare* 'Purpureum'), which can be harvested by the chefs or left to flower for bees and butterflies. This resolution of the possibilities works well as a transition from gardens to fields, with enough structure to transition the seasons and with plants blurring the division between garden and farm.

To buffer the high-traffic Campo patios and kitchen service area from the adjacent North Field Casitas, an evergreen was the best option. But most evergreens are slow-growing. Afghan pines (*Pinus brutia eldarica*) were planted because they are adapted to clay soils, fast-growing, and available in larger sizes. They are also one of the most drought and heat tolerant of the conifers. While they repeat the feel and resiny scent of the other pine species at Los Poblanos, they take less water and respond to the increasing heat with equanimity.

The Field Suites, north of the Campo multi-

Raised beds and pétanque seen from the Bar Campo patio firepit. Echoing rows of crops in the fields, the raised beds east of Campo serve several purposes. They are strong architectural elements and stage a beautiful mix of plants, attracting the attention of human guests as well as pollinators, which improve crop productivity. They are also a seasonally changing foreground for the mutable mountain view. Photograph by the author.

use space, had less demanding programming. The initial idea was to use the field that runs between them as a trial field for botanicals that might be distilled as hydrosols for body care products. One option was clary sage (*Salvia sclarea*), an herb I had little experience with but wanted to include in the landscape partly for its healing and culinary uses and also because it is strikingly beautiful and well adapted. Clary sage grows clusters of large, velvety silver leaves and tall stems of showy hooded flowers, which may be either white or white-blushed rose pink. I also thought Penny Rembe might find

it a striking addition to the floral arrangements she places throughout the inn. Later I learned from growing the plant that its scent, which is not noticeable in the open air, is less desirable in cut flowers in enclosed spaces. Los Poblanos distiller Jamie Lord dryly confirms that there's a good reason a few drops of the essential oils that give clary sage its potency and odor go a long way in product formulas.

The seed was too expensive to experiment with in an entire field, and the plant is short-lived and would need replanting every few years, so we instead used it as filler, in spots where it would be easy to harvest for distilling. Sourcing plants at the time proved difficult, and we were about to table the idea when, as often happens among gardeners, a friend said she had plants self-sowing copiously in her backyard. Could she pot some up for me? Instead of signaling potential weediness, the fact that clary sage self-sows readily in our climate was good news, made even better by the knowledge that every generation of native or naturalized seedlings is liable to be more adapted to local growing conditions. So the sample clary sage planted in the new landscape is a pass-along plant, given to one gardener by another. Whenever I walk past them, I thank my friend Margaret for the plants and for the opportunity to learn about them firsthand.

Prairie Garden Pollinator Habitat

On the Olin master plan, the open space between the northernmost rows of Field Suites was labeled "botanicals." This was space to play with plants that might be used to distill hydrosols. Challenged by Matt Rembe to create an informal, agrarian, and potentially edible landscape that would be beautiful, be easy to maintain, and transform into crop space when necessary, the team decided to seed the north fields with a mix of native grasses and wildflowers as a prairie groundcover. The grasses—blue grama (*Bouteloua gracilis*), alkali sacaton (*Sporobolus airiodes*), and little bluestem (*Schizachyrium scoparium*)—are the structure of the prairie. In our dry climate, when seeded as a groundcover, these grasses transition from short hummocks of soft leaves in late spring to a filigree of soft green and pale purple by midsummer, when seed heads form on knee-high thready stems. The grasses are especially interesting when backlit by the rising or setting sun. The grama and sacaton cure in shades of pale tan, and

Clary sage (Salvia sclarea) is a striking plant with large fuzzy leaves and tall spikes of hooded flowers. It self-sows readily and has been spreading along the west side of the north Field Suites, providing plenty of distillation material for Los Poblanos body care products. Photograph by the author.

The wildflowers and native grasses in the prairie groundcover support wildlife on many levels. The flowers supply excellent bee pollen and nectar, while the grasses are essential forage for caterpillars and the seeds that are a feast for both resident and migratory songbirds. Photograph by the author.

as the days grow shorter and the nights chillier, the bluestem (*Schizachyrium scoparium*) turns brilliant copper red because the variety 'Blaze' was planted. Dew glistening on the soft grass blades on a summer morning or the sun slanting through the seed heads in autumn and winter adds a glow to this tribute to native desert grassland. While there are subtle seasonal changes throughout the year, with its warm tawny cover and bounty of seeds for resident and migratory birds, it is outstanding as a landscape feature from September through winter.

To naturally improve the soil microflora and supply the grasses with nitrogen, purple prairie clover (*Dalea purpurea*) was added to the mix. When this wildflower blooms, it adds a rose purple haze to the field in summer, but it is similar to the grasses in height and texture, so it blends in inconspicuously when not in bloom. The seeds of all these natives are a feast for songbirds. Prairie clover produces excellent bee pollen and nectar, while the plants themselves are essential forage for caterpillars, which become beautiful butterflies: "flowers with wings." This is a temporary planting, until the space is needed for another crop, enriching the soil as it grows, and is another example of the layers of value provided by the careful use of water. Once the seeding is balanced and well established, prairie groundcover requires little maintenance, except for mowing in spring to remove the previous year's thatch. The clippings may be used as mulch to suppress weeds elsewhere or composted to add fiber to the annual crop fields.

Los Poblanos director of horticulture Wes Brittenham inherited this new prairie and an adjacent field that was not seeded in the initial landscape project. He continues the tale: "Prior to seeding the native grasses and wildflowers, I noted how the then free-range alpacas tended to hang out in the areas needing reseeding and in so doing disturbed

Alpaca tractoring. Alpacas are multitalented animals. They entertain young guests while they disturb the soil lightly and prepare it for seeding. Photograph by Wes Brittenham.

the soil very lightly. Knowing I was not going to amend or till the soil, I employed what I call 'alpaca tractoring.' By moving their water source, I was able to coax the alpacas from section to section, seeding in the disturbed areas a section at a time." The techniques employed in the gardens of Los Poblanos are organic in every sense of the term.

Changing Cultural Expectations

Out of necessity, there is a cultural shift in attitudes in both landscape architecture and agriculture, a change in thinking from exploitation to resiliency. Declines in populations of bees and other pollinators have made it imperative to think of gardens and farm fields as ecosystems and to work holistically to sustain both. As Dennis McGlade notes, "If gardening and agriculture are about using plants to humanity's ends, are these other ways of utilizing plants (reforestation, urban forestry, and bioremediation) a new form of gardening or agriculture? We're not harvesting for fuel, fiber, or food, but we're employing plants to renew the environment, as they can the human spirit."

The gardens of Los Poblanos have always been and continue to be a center for experimentation and adaptation. In the Simms era, the goals were to expand the diversity of crops that could be grown profitably in the valley. The goals today are similar, while the plant choices differ as human tastes and climate shifts revise decisions. The 2020 master plan for the village of Los Ranchos includes as priorities "relatively low density and diversified residential land uses; continued agricultural uses including animal husbandry; preservation of historic or archeologically significant buildings and features; and preservation of traditional land use patterns and identifiable familiar vernacular characteristics," including acequias and heritage trees. Los Poblanos continues to be a center for spreading an ecology-based land ethic into the community, in a very appropriate way, returning to the land ethic of the first gardeners here.

In 2006 Nancy Kinyanjui came to Los Poblanos Inn to help the Rembes manage the increasingly complex tasks of running this historic property. She ended her stay as general manager in 2017. Originally from Kenya, Nancy had a combination of assets, including an education in biology and design and experience in the hotel and inn industry. She has many wonderful memories from her time at Los Poblanos: "Imagine my surprise when I started working at a farm in the desert that has a rich his-

tory of flood irrigation and a memorable network of acequias. No matter how busy I was at the inn, I am happy to say that I would often find time to sneak a few moments on irrigation day to take off my shoes and stand in the crisp water on the lawn."

With lavender products gaining markets, Stephen Humphry was added to the team to manage the Farm Shop. Both Nancy and Stephen quickly became extended family members, and as shared work became shared lives, they celebrated their wedding at Los Poblanos, an international affair with family from Kenya attending. Nancy remembers, "I've always admired the bold, brave colors of marigolds. . . . When I decided to make marigold garlands for my wedding at Los Poblanos, I enlisted the help of Farmer Ric, who agreed to set aside three rows in the front field to grow them. After work, often in the dark with a headlamp, I would harvest the flowers to string and dry into garlands, hanging them up in the lavender barn. I loved seeing these flowers pop up in the field years later."

On visits to Kenya, Stephen began working with local craftspeople, especially woodcarvers, importing their carved utensils to market at Los Poblanos. (There is something so appealing about the small carved wooden spoons that a few seem to follow me home almost every time I visit the Farm Shop.) Seeds of ideas germinated in these fertile minds, and the regenerative land ethic that blossomed in Nancy and Stephen at Los Poblanos—the belief that care of the land benefits the whole community—and the skills they developed there eventually traveled halfway around the planet with them. In 2017 Nancy and Stephen moved to Nairobi. There, with Nancy's sister Susie, they founded Provisions Kenya.

Like Los Poblanos, Provisions Kenya is dedicated to marketing products of local farmers and

Ducks in the pond. Like ripples in the global pond, Los Poblanos is part of a much larger effort to restore balance and resilience to agriculture and the planet. Photograph by Wes Brittenham.

mutually beneficial actions spurred by mycorrhizae-of-the-mind and good ideas going global.

Sources, and an Invitation to Dig Deeper

Apiarist. "Mobile Beekeeping." *Apiarist*, February 17, 2017, https://www.theapiarist.org/tag/anton-znidersic.

Berry, Wendell. "Private Property and the Common Wealth." *Wild Earth* 5 (Fall 1995):6.

Gould, Kevin S. "Nature's Swiss Army Knife: The Diverse Protective Roles of Anthocyanins in Leaves." *Journal of Biomedicine and Biotechnology* 5:314–20, https://doi.org/10.1155/S1110724304406147.

Haiying Cui, Xuejing Zhang, Hui Zhou, Chengting Zhao, and Lin Lin. "Antimicrobial Activity and Mechanisms of *Salvia Sclarea* Essential Oil." *Botanical Studies* 56 (December 2015):16, https://www.ncbi.nlm.nih.gov/pmc/articles/PMC5432889.

Kinyanjui, Nancy. "Sister Proprietors: Provisions Kenya." *Spin Off*, May 28, 2021, https://spinoffmagazine.com/sister-proprietors-provisions-kenya.

Provisions Kenya, https://www.provisions.co.ke.

Schwartz, Allen. "The Best of a Langstroth and a Slovenian Hive Means No Lifting!" *Bee Culture*, January 3, 2018, https://www.beeculture.com/langstroth-slovenian-hybrid-hive.

Seiler, Gerald, and Chao-Chien Jan. "Sunflower." Sunflower and Plant Biology Research: Fargo, ND, April 1, 2010, https://www.ars.usda.gov/research/publications/publication/?seqNo115=229735.

Tijeras Creek Remediation Project, https://www.facebook.com/pg/TijerasCreekProject.

artisans, but Nancy and Stephen were dismayed to find imported synthetic yarns flooding the Kenyan market. Now they are on a mission to reverse the synthetic trend and to promote beautiful natural fibers by selling Rift Valley Yarn, sheared from Kenyan sheep and carded, spun, and dyed by a women's cooperative in Nairobi. They are also developing partnerships in the farming community, with the goal of making regenerative agriculture lucrative, and are encouraging farmers to preserve wild pastures for sheep grazing and rare bird habitat rather than planting monocultural exotic pasture grasses. Their decade at Los Poblanos is a story much larger than Nancy and Stephen or any of the other Los Poblanos farmer alumni who are now managing their own growing projects. Regenerative agriculture is the resilient result of an ever-expanding network of

Pétanque court dining during the pandemic. Serving people in the fresh air of the gardens was a great asset during the pandemic and meshed perfectly with the overall goals of Los Poblanos. Several patios and portal spaces were adapted to winter dining; the pétanque court accommodated overflow. As the pandemic eased, many guests still opted to dine alfresco. Photograph by the author.

CHAPTER 7

Coming Full Circle, 2021 and Onward

Plants tell their stories not by what they say but by what they do. . . .
Plants teach in a universal language: food.

—Robin Wall Kimmerer, biologist and member of the Citizen Potawatomi Nation

Those who had inhabited this land, who spoke the language of myth
and metaphor and enacted it in ceremony and art, meant different things
by "discovery," "growth" and "beginning."

—Betty Fussell, **The Story of Corn**

Today's Los Poblanos is a working farm as well as an ecotourism and agritourism destination: a forty-five-guest room inn on a twenty-five-acre lavender farm, the setting for memorable farm-to-table culinary adventures, personal retreats, weddings and other special events, and wellness immersions. It is a restorative resource for people in the local community as well as for visitors from all over the world, with guest experiences carefully curated by the Rembe family and staff. Their dedication is written in the landscape, whether they're preserving the history and integrity of the site, maintaining agricultural ties such as acequia irrigation, or making Los Poblanos a resiliently profitable enterprise. There is a rich story to be told by tracing the evolution of the early plantings, those that have continued to thrive through changing times, and new plantings that are now adapting to a hotter, drier climate. It is a tale of the how, when, where, and why of choosing and coaxing plants to grow. While the quarter century between 1994 and 2019 witnessed the greatest shift in paradigm, the gardens of Los Poblanos have remained true to their cultural antecedents— so much so that today the ornamental gardens and agricultural landscape are blended, often blurred with no distinct boundaries.

The land on which Los Poblanos has grown has experienced an evolution: from unsettled river floodplain to lightly settled and cultivated pueblos having a reciprocal relationship with the ecology, from the small subsistence farming that introduced many new edible plants to amalgamation into the many-thousand-acre Los Poblanos Ranch, the country place of Albert and Ruth Simms in the early in the twentieth century, when the introduction of exotic plant species was considered a means of civilizing the desert. The Simms also worked to increase agricultural productivity by experimentation and careful management. But with changing times, Los Poblanos was gradually whittled down to its current twenty-five acres by suburban expansion.

This seems to have always been a fortuitous place. Dividing and then reuniting the twenty-five acres, the Rembe family respectfully preserves the historic architecture and engages in a distinctly regenerative approach to land use. They have avoided large-lot development eroding the remaining farmland and are finding ways to return the land to ecological productivity that are culturally respectful and economically feasible in the twenty-first century. The preservation strategies are market-driven, honoring the past by gently using the historic buildings to reveal the past to guests in a direct way—with no velvet ropes protecting a fossilized era but with access to an eclectic library, walls hung with photographs from the 1930s and 1940s ranch and dairy, and tea service and harvest feasts on the Grand Portal at La Quinta.

The changes in the gardens of Los Poblanos reflect the evolution of American landscape architecture toward an ecologically more resilient model and a growing appreciation for locally produced food. Internationally, ecology became a rigorous science in the late 1800s with the emergence of evolutionary biology, but landscape ecology as a subset of landscape architecture has taken nearly a century longer to be integrated into landscape design practice. At its best, landscape architecture is a collaborative discipline. Depending on the nature of the place and the project, hydrologists, civil and storm water engineers, horticulturists, urban planners, irrigation specialists, psychologists, foresters, wetland or dryland ecologists, land artists, and architects may all have significant roles to play in the design.

The whole earth image, the blue planet floating in a dark sea of space as seen from the Apollo 8 mission in 1968, seemed to capture the human consciousness in a way that even the experience of the most awe-inspiring places on that blue orb could not. In 1969 the publication of Ian McHarg's *Design with Nature* was certainly a pivotal moment in recognition of the opportunity to design places in collaboration with natural systems rather than in opposition to them. Since then, many landscape architects have elaborated on that simple idea, working out the complexities of how to apply the beauty and value of natural systems to private and public gardens. Much more remains to be done.

In the gardens of Los Poblanos, the evolution is far from over. As a small, well-established business, Los Poblanos was nimble in the early 2020s in the face of COVID-19 quarantines, closures, limited reopening, and finally the vaccinated blossoming, all the while keeping core staff and guests as healthy and happy as dynamic uncertainty allows. The gardens of Los Poblanos were a great asset in moving people outdoors, and the gardens are a very real and perhaps now more keenly appreciated health benefit, both physically and mentally, to staff and visitors. The pandemic forced the cancellation of eighty weddings that had been scheduled for 2020, with eighty disappointing letters and phone calls made to the brides and grooms.

Some staff had to be laid off as the pandemic wore on in 2021 and the Rembe family and core management team reassessed the present and future of Los Poblanos. Lavender products expanded to include a lavender hand sanitizer, which was difficult to keep in stock. As a reflection of health care empathy, since doctors have been in the house in both the Simms and Rembe eras, thousands of bottles of sanitizer were distributed free to local hospitals as a thank-you to people caring for COVID patients and to the Navajo Nation and Pueblo communities, who were particularly challenged by the pandemic. The chefs at Campo prepared carry-out family dinners, and as the growing season progressed, the farmers initiated a socially distanced produce stand to spread the fresh bounty of the fields to the neighborhood and beyond. Pickup times for meals ordered online were staggered, yet the lines of cars waiting for meals along the shaded driveway sometimes moved slowly as the demand was so great. The wait under the elm canopy was an opportunity to relax and think positive thoughts, with time to examine the tessellated bark and the massiveness of the trees and to consider their longevity while catching glimpses of alpacas and sandhill cranes, which were blissfully unaware that the world had shifted on its axis. An amazing meal was the ultimate reward.

The slower pace forced by the pandemic was an opportunity to rethink programming and adapt to new constraints. When state health mandates allowed, outdoor dining resumed, with tables extending out into the pétanque courts. While the plants were still dormant in winter, the view of the Sandia Mountains, which seem closer when frosted with an increasingly rare snowfall, was a great backdrop for a delicious meal. Lingering through a spectacular New Mexico sunset, warmed by propane heaters and *chimineas*—small, portable wood-burning fireplaces traditionally made of clay or sheet metal—seemed to visitors to be more a privilege than a concession to COVID.

Focus on Farm Foods

To keep as many staff members as possible working during the pandemic and to rehire as quickly as possible, pivotal decisions had to be made. One of the first was to limit the size and number of future events to concentrate on guests at the inn and Campo. New programs such as afternoon tea on the Grand Portal at La Quinta allowed the kitchen to shine while sharing a bit of the history of Los Poblanos with guests. Serving people in the fresh air of the gardens was a great asset during the pandemic and meshed perfectly with the overall goals of the place. Scheduled meals and teas, instead of one-time events, made the quantities of fresh produce and other supplies grown and purchased more predictable in a business where inconsistency is the norm. This in turn gave local farmers who contribute to the quality of meals at Los Poblanos a firmer basis for planning crops and a more consistent income. Processing and preserving overly abundant produce not only prevents waste and therefore economic losses but also keeps skilled chefs employed and able to train new help.

The saving grace of e-commerce led Los Poblanos to apply to the New Mexico Economic Development Department for Local Economic Development Act (LEDA) funding. Los Poblanos would move some of its lavender and food processing and storage off-site to a nine-thousand-square-foot warehouse just north of downtown Albuquerque to greatly expand its capacity to support local agriculture. Governor Michelle Lujan Grisham said, "This is a win-win for New Mexico manufacturing and agriculture. I'm excited about this expansion and what it means for farmers, ranchers, and growers all across our state. We will continue to seek out opportunities with partners like Los Poblanos to boost locally grown food and job creation."

Los Poblanos has invested in new warehouse space for processing lavender and food products. The site is a renovated tractor company building, seen here under construction in 1948. The move allows Los Poblanos to increase production without greater impact on the historic property. PA1980.185.346, Albuquerque Museum, gift of Albuquerque National Bank.

Ironically, this expansion off-site helps preserve the rural serenity at Los Poblanos as it deepens partnerships with the agricultural community, granting a greater measure of economic stability to growers. If Los Poblanos can buy, process, and market more, New Mexican farmers can grow more, while back at the inn life goes on at a pace that respects and preserves the culture and guest experience.

The easing of restrictions took place at the height of spring 2021, when guests breathed in the intoxicating fragrances of the Rose Greely Garden and noshed in the shade of tree canopies and sunbrellas. The farmers and gardeners had been busy with the seasonal routines of planting early crops and planning for succession in the fields, pruning woody plants, and cutting back weathered perennials. They removed declining lavender in the fields, preparing the land for planting with well-rooted lavender cuttings waiting in the greenhouse, along with trays of vegetable seedlings and flower starts for the cutting garden.

Sadly, the blossoming of a new spring was also a time of great loss, as Armin Rembe, patri-

Greenhouse waiting for spring. Packed with potential, the greenhouses at Los Poblanos span the seasons, allowing fresh food to be harvested year-round and new crops to be given a jump-start in a climate where erratic frosts often shorten the growing season. Photograph by Wes Brittenham.

Armin and Penny Rembe enjoy a courtyard in the Field Suites in 2018. Photograph by Sergio Salvador.

Flooding the three sisters and camp followers. Maize, beans, and squash are crop siblings that supported early valley farmers and continue to provide for guests at Los Poblanos. Devil's claw (*Proboscidea parviflora*), in the foreground, and sunflowers are camp followers in this diverse maize, beans, and squash field planted in 2019. Photograph by Wes Brittenham.

arch of the family and steward of Los Poblanos for forty-five fulfilling years, passed away in late April 2021. His last days were spent in the place he loved most, surrounded by family. His legacy—the love of learning and dedication to place and people—is at the core of Los Poblanos, in the water and soil and alive in the next generation of caretakers.

Not only does life go on, but it also bursts forth as the earth warms, and farmers and gardeners have to be ready to deal with the surge of new growth. Farm and kitchen collaboration—planning crops to fill menus—is the work of Wes Brittenham, director of horticulture, and the chefs in the Campo kitchens, who gleefully engage in growing and preparing the highest-quality food possible. They meet often to review crops nearing harvest, assess the current season's scheduling, and fine-tune planting scenarios for next season. Wes says, "I have been a gardener and farmer all of my life. My father was a farmer and his father before him, on and on. The chefs have deepened my knowledge and appreciation of how, what, and why we grow, and I'm grateful for the continuing education."

Rio Grande Valley Cuisine

The Los Poblanos culinary team's farm-to-table philosophy and the Rembes' land, culture, and historic preservation ethic have matured as Rio Grande Valley cuisine, the signature of Campo. At the heart of the local celebration of food that the Rio Grande provides is the challenging idea that food is seasonal, a gift to be grateful for, and a means of maintaining a resilient community. Jonathan Perno, the executive chef from 2008 through 2021, greatly influenced the coming of age of the Rio Grande Valley cuisine concept. His views on carnivory reflect the values that underlie the bounty at Campo: raising animals humanely, slaughtering quickly and painlessly, and using as many byproducts as possible. His words bring to mind John Barlow's excellent culinary travelogue

Field meeting with (left to right) Maxfield Bervig, farm manager; Jhelle Gonzales-Duran, kitchen manager and food facility manager; Christopher Bethoney, head chef; and Wes Brittenham, director of horticulture. Close communication field-to-kitchen keeps the quality of produce at its peak when served to guests. The teams meets regularly to check the development of crops and to plan future harvesting. Photograph by the author.

Everything but the Squeal: Eating the Whole Hog in Northern Spain, a book that relishes the journey of discovery that can accompany every meal.

The cultural link between Rio Grande Valley cuisine and whole hog respect for and enjoyment of food is strong, but the succulent fruit and vegetables only a farm field away are the heart of the seasonal menus. The current team of chefs brings experiences gleaned at Le Cordon Bleu, the Culinary Institute of America, and the Ayurvedic Institute. Some have apprenticed with skilled chefs in fine restaurants across the United States and Europe, including Chef Perno at Campo. They work with Los Poblanos farmers as well as other local growers to meld cultural traditions and flavors with locally grown produce at the seasonal peak of flavor.

The corn grown in the gardens of Los Poblanos varies from year to year but is likely to include

strawberry popcorn, Hopi pink and blue, Oaxacan green, and other heirloom varieties from Native Seeds Search and Baker Seeds. The Zuni corn, from a single ear given to Wes Brittenham, can be traced back through many generations in the same Zuni family. For a thousand years, Native peoples have shared the bounty of their crops, and the tradition continues. Corn is planted in the fields east of Campo, within view of the restaurant windows and patios. To make a direct link from field to table, a roasting pit was built along the access drive to the kitchen. The pit is eight feet across and five feet deep, lined with plaster made of on-site clay mixed with manure and straw, with stones set in the plaster. A lid was made by removing the bottom of a circular galvanized stock tank and attaching crossbars as handles. Diners can watch their corn being harvested, roasted, and delivered to their table, a three-act drama with a delicious denouement. Cornfield to roaster to table in less than one hundred footsteps could be a new record for farm-to-fork dining. Guests in the nearby Field Suites can be seduced by the aromas of their next meal.

The roaster is large enough to accommodate large cuts of meat and harkens back to a cultural tradition in New Mexico, the *matanza*, roasting a whole hog to share with friends and relatives. This was once common in the colder months and still takes place in the valley; it also provides fond memories for ranch hands and farmers from the Simms era at Los Poblanos. An adobe *horno*, a beehive-shaped oven traditionally used for bread baking but that also can yield succulent roast turkeys and geese, is yet to be built. Making meal preparation a drama to be enjoyed by guests and chefs is part of the immersion experience here.

Santo Domingo tobacco (*Nicotiana rustica*), traditionally used in rituals to bring rain, is grown at the request of Native chefs and is steeped to use

A roasting pit formalizes the local tradition of the matanza, when families and neighbors gather to feast on their seasonal bounty. Photograph by Wes Brittenham.

Removing roasted corn is part of the Los Poblanos field–to–fork experience. The drama of fire adds to the dining experience. Photograph by Wes Brittenham.

as a carefully managed biological pest control as well. The farm and gardens overlap in the dominance of fruit trees and shrubs, including plums, figs, pomegranates, herbs, and cardoons (*Cynara cardunculus*), in the gardens that surround the Field Suites near Campo. From the older portions of the garden, daylily buds and flowers (*Hemerocallis* cultivars) are harvested along with heirloom apples and mulberries. Seeds of nasturtium (*Tropaeolum* cultivars) are pickled and used as capers; the flowers and young leaves are used as garnishes with a distinctly peppery taste. Bar Campo also has close ties to the gardens, with mixologists and farmers collaborating to create fresh organic cocktails using lavender simple syrup, bitters, cynar, and amari as well as other farm produce.

Distillation: From Lavender Harvest to Lavender Oil and Hydrosol

At Los Poblanos, high summer is an exceptionally active time, when the lavender is harvested and distilled fresh or dried for later processing. Distiller Jamie Lord prefers to work with freshly cut lavender, one hundred pounds at a time, in copper alembic stills in the outdoor distillation shed. A visit to the distilling shed is itself an intoxicating experience. With trugs of fresh-cut lavender, a drying rack loaded with more lavender, and a chaste tree (*Vitex agnus-castus*) in full bloom and buzzing with bees, the air is saturated with scent. Jamie loads the fresh lavender into the base and column of the still, grouts the seams with rye flour paste,

In copper alembic vessels, hundred-pound batches of fresh lavender are distilled, one at a time, until the annual crop is processed. Photograph by the author.

Distiller Jamie Lord prefers to work with freshly cut lavender, one hundred pounds at a time, in the copper alembic stills in the outdoor distillation shed. But to meet demand, distillation continues long after the harvest season has ended. Photograph by the author.

and fills the base of the still with well water early in the day. It takes a bit of time for the water to heat and for the steam to begin drawing oils from the flowers and stems. The condenser coils are surrounded by cold water, which cools the steam as it moves through them. By midday, the condensed hydrosol and oil are steadily trickling out. Since the lavender oil is lighter than the hydrosol, it rises to the top of the glass separator, a bulb-like flask with a spout at the bottom. The heavier hydrosol sinks to the bottom of the separator and into collecting jugs. Once the batch is exhausted, the still is gently cleaned with citric acid, and the process begins again. Load, steam, cool, clean, and repeat until the crop is distilled, the essence of summer captured.

Copper alembic stills have been used for hundreds of years because of their durability, their beauty, and the quality of the oils and hydrosols they produce. Copper is an excellent conductor of heat, critical to the even heating and cooling of the product. It is anticorrosive and antibacterial. Unlike aluminum or stainless steel, copper draws sulfur from the plant material, crystalizing it on the inside of the still, so the distillate is pure and clean. While lavender distillation is a focus in summer and autumn, Jamie and her team also distill orange oil and hydrosol from kitchen waste. Breakfast orange peels and pulp are upcycled into oil and hydrosol, and because the distilling process breaks down the material so well, the dross from the still can be composted. Likewise, the spent lavender is dried and used as bedding in the chicken yard before it too is composted. With nature as a model, there is no waste. Jamie began distilling lavender as Armin Rembe's apprentice and has been working the stills for eight years. Always game to try new plants in the stills, she has distilled pine, rose, and other flowers from the gardens for oils and hydrosols and has distilled a tasty cordial from the fruits of the Russian hawthorn trees (*Crataegus ambigua*) growing in the La Quinta parking medians.

Matt Rembe describes the commitment: "Our entire team is engaged on issues of the land and sustainability. We dedicate a lot of time to supporting local nonprofits dedicated to food issues, water issues, education, historic preservation, tourism, and economic development. New Mexico is a state with so many needs, and we're in a unique position where we can add value to these conversations as well as learn from them." Popular on-site programs include tours and demonstrations to raise public awareness of regenerative agricultural practices, native landscaping to support pollinators and wildlife, and water conservation practices in food production. The team at Los Poblanos challenges themselves by participating in conferences and workshops on innovative farming practices, and they work with local volunteers at the organic farm during the growing and harvesting seasons to sow the seeds of these ideas and techniques in the community.

Adaptive Reuse: Post-Covid Wellness and Lavender Applied

The historic hacienda at Los Poblanos is once again being adapted to serve a new purpose. John Gaw Meem set a standard when he designed this space, complete with a handmade tile that reads "Dedicada a la Vida Generosa." (Dedicated to a Generous Life). While some things change irrevocably, the path to well-being can be simple: a slow pace,

Renovation in the placita. Reworking the beds, tilework, and paving in the placita was part of repurposing the historic hacienda and the new wellness spa. Photograph by the author.

Hacienda Spa transformation. The rebirth of the historic placita as the Hacienda Spa begins a new phase in wellness in the gardens of Los Poblanos. An all-encompassing dedication to well-being that extends far beyond lavender body products prompted the transformation of the hacienda into a well-appointed spa. This is farm to massage table at its finest. Photograph by Douglas Merriam.

caring for the people around you, breathing in the fragrances of lavender and rose, sage and pine, and hearing the call of geese dropping into the pond, bees intent on honey-making, and songbirds nesting in the cottonwoods. What began in the 1930s as the residence of Albert and Ruth Simms became the home of Dr. Albert Simms II and his family in the 1960s and the home of the Rembe family in the 1970s. At the turn of the new century, it was transformed into Los Poblanos Inn. Evan Geisler, architect and project coordinator at Geisler Projects, designed the next transformation. Spaces that were once family bedrooms and then guest rooms are now spa treatment rooms, where botanical products made from plants grown in the gardens nearby are used to comfort and restore guests.

The historic placita was refurbished in 2020. The well-established Lady Banks roses (*Rosa banksia lutea*) remain, yellow trumpet vine (*Campsis radicans f. fulva*) still drapes the portales, and the more restrained chocolate vine (*Akebia quinata*) climbs one of the north posts. Wes Brittenham describes his thought process in selecting plants for the refurbished beds: "I carefully considered the plants as I reimagined the courtyard landscape at the hacienda. The blue calibrachoa in the west raised beds reference the petunias in snippets of film from the Simms days. The yellow knockout roses (*Rosa* hybrid 'Sunny Knockout') pay homage to Rose Greely and Penny Rembe's love of roses, and the color of bloom complements the Lady Banks. The burkwood viburnums reference not only the vertical shrubs they replaced but their historic use in other gardens. . . . The winter jasmine (*Jasminum nudiflorum*) appears elsewhere on the property but excels in my own home garden, as do the northern sea oats (*Chasmanthium latifolium*) in a microclimate that is very close to the exposure of the courtyard, hence the decision to use them." These are plants with sensory depth. Spicy early spring viburnum, light citrus roses, and the gentle rustling of the grasses all add to the experience of quiet calm. The ghost of Rose Greely is nodding her approval.

Wellness yurt. In a niche carved into the wild garden, an open but protected space for yoga practice under a canopy of trees seemed a natural evolution. Birdsong and the whisper of the breeze through the trees are the calming accompaniment to breathing and stretching exercises. Photograph by the author.

Farther out in the gardens, a yoga platform and yurt have mushroomed in a niche carved out of the wild garden, creating an open but protected space for yoga practice under the canopy of trees. Birdsong and the whisper of the breeze through the pines are the calming accompaniment to breathing and stretching exercises. As construction of the yurt proceeded, while removing Siberian elm and other invasive seedlings in the wild garden, Brittenham looked at the way sun filters and angles through the tree canopy during the day and considered what accent plants might be added to create focal vignettes for yoga practitioners. Wes's philosophy of restoration in the gardens of Los Poblanos is not to harken back to a past time here. Climate change has proven the landscape restoration model to be a fool's errand. Instead, he opts "to find the bones of what it was and strip away the debris of years," of plants self-sowing and bird-planting, to see what is possible now that might weather into the future. Weedy volunteers cue a gardener about

Dry Rio. Climate change is challenging farmers everywhere. Along the Rio Grande, seeing the riverbed dry is sobering. Accepting water as a gift to share and use wisely is the way to a resilient future. Photograph by Hunter Ten Broeck.

small changes that accumulate over time; garden debris is data accumulating over time. What grows with minimal assistance shines a light on what a space has become and what it might still be. Los Poblanos, it seems, casts a kind of light against the obscurity of the future.

> Before we talk about the future,
> we need to talk about the past.
> This land is marked with stories.
> They are in the washes after it rains,
> in the small undulations,
> in the rasp of desert breath.
> —Autumn Bernhardt, Indigenous poet,
> lawyer, teacher, and rancher

Sources, and an Invitation to Dig Deeper

Baker Seeds, https://www.rareseeds.com.

Barlow, John. *Everything but the Squeal: Eating the Whole Hog in Northern Spain*. New York: Farrar, Straus and Giroux, 2008.

Bernhardt, Autumn. "Before We Talk about Grazing," in *Grazing the Fire: Poetry of Rangeland Science*, edited by María E. Fernández-Giménez. Fort Collins, CO: Wolverine Farm Publishing, 2018.

Brittenham, Wes. Conversations with author, 2021.

Ecological Landscape Alliance. "Native Plants." Ecological Landscape Alliance, 2022, https://www.ecolandscaping.org/category/designing-ecological-landscapes/native-plants.

Fussell, Betty. *The Story of Corn*. New York: Alfred A Knopf, 1992.

Kimmerer, Robin Wall. *Braiding Sweetgrass: Indigenous Wisdom, Scientific Knowledge, and the Teachings of Plants*. Minneapolis: Milkweed Editions, 2013.

Lord, Jamie. Conversation with author, 2021.

McHarg, Ian. *Design with Nature*. New York: American Museum of Natural History, 1969.

Native Seeds Search, https://www.nativeseeds.org.

Perno, Jonathan. Conversation with author, 2021.

Underhill, Ruth. *Life in the Pueblos*. Santa Fe: Ancient City Press, 1991.

GLOSSARY

acequias: Formalized irrigation channels of Moorish origins that Spaniards brought from the Old World to divert and redistribute Rio Grande waters more extensively and predictably.

allée: A narrow lane bordered by parallel rows of trees. The Los Poblanos allée is the main driveway.

bosque: Woodland habitat adjacent to a river or stream in the southwestern United States, possible because of the shallow water table.

camp followers: Edible or medicinal plants that cropped up in the cultivated fields of early Native farmers. These "volunteers" were used along with the intended crops, a gift of nature.

canales: Traditional roof drains common on flat-roofed buildings. Typically they are chutes made of galvanized sheet metal that extend a foot or more beyond the roof parapet and drop rainwater directly to the ground below.

chimineas: Small, portable fireplaces used on patios for comfort on chilly spring and autumn evenings.

curanderismo: The art and science of traditional healing. A curandera/curandero is a traditional healer well-versed in the local pharmacopeia.

cynar: An Italian bitter aperitif made with thirteen herbs and unique in having artichoke as its base.

ecology: The study of the relationships between living organisms, their life processes and adaptations, and their physical environment.

encomienda system: A Spanish colonial labor system that rewarded conquistadors and soldiers with land and forced labor or tribute in necessary goods from the Native peoples the colonizers dispossessed.

ferme ornee: An ornamental and working farm where the pleasure garden, kitchen garden, and surrounding farmland are parts of a coherent whole.

horno: A traditional outdoor oven built of adobe, usually on a larger square base. The beehive-shaped oven has an arched opening for loading wood fuel and a vent for smoke to escape when the main opening is sealed.

hydrosol: An herbal distillate.

landrace plants: Particularly vigorous, productive plants adapted to the local soil, climate, and growing conditions. Unlike cultivars selected for characteristics such as color, flower size, and form, landrace plants are selected for greater genetic diversity, which allows them to adapt to climate changes more quickly.

Mudejar: Architectural and landscape features borrowed from Islamic traditions widely used in Spain in the twelfth to fifteenth centuries.

mycorrhizae: Microbial life in healthy soils that forms associations with plants, extending their root systems to tap a much greater soil area. The relationship is usually symbiotic: mycorrhizae receive starches from plants in return for the increased absorptive capacity they give the plants.

parterre: A patterned planting of small evergreen plants, often framing beds planted with colorful annuals or perennials. Meant to be viewed from above, parterres are usually placed on the flat ground of a lower terrace.

placita: A small plaza that is more intimate than a larger public plaza.

querencia: Devotion to a place as an essential part of life; derived from the Spanish verb *querer*, meaning "to desire."

terrones: Blocks of soil and roots cut from marshland, dried, and used as earthen bricks in construction.

trug: A shallow, wide gardening basket used to carry produce from the field. Contemporary trugs are often made of light, flexible, brightly colored plastic.

xeriscape: An adaptive landscape design style developed in response to western water shortages. Begun by Denver Water, xeriscape (from the Greek *xeros*, meaning "dry") includes reducing lawn areas, using native and arid-adapted plants in well-designed gardens, concentrating higher water use near the home, using mulches to conserve soil moisture and improve soil health, and maintaining landscapes appropriately.

zaguan: A traditional entryway in the southwestern United States and Mexico, typically a covered space with a gateway wide enough to be a coach entrance but also having a pedestrian doorway. The zaguan leads directly to a central courtyard, and all rooms in the home open into the courtyard.

Index

ivy: Boston ivy (*Parthenocissus tricuspidata*), 102, 108; English ivy (*Hedera helix*), 36, 81, 102, 108

Jackman clematis, 49
Jackson, J. B., 27
Jacobson, Jacob Peter, 41
Japanese garden, 80
Japanese maple (*Acer palmatum*), 55
Jefferson, Thomas, 17, 29, 63
Jekyll, Gertrude, 31
Jemez Mountains, clear-cutting of forest and grazing in, 16
Jensen, Jens, 1, 30
Jicarilla Apaches, 14
Jobs, Steve, 5
Johnson, Albert and Bessie, 32
joint fir (*Ephedra torreyana*), 11
The Journal of a Santa Fe Trader, Gregg article in (1844), 15
jujube (*Ziziphus jujuba*), 38, 101, *101*, 123, *123, 124*
Jujube Vinegar (recipe), 124
'Julia Child' shrub roses (*Rosa* hybrids*)*, 122
juniper (*Juniperus* spp.), 80, 105: alligator juniper (*Juniperus deppeana*), 37; blue junipers (*Juniperus chinesis* spp.), 81; eastern red cedar (*Juniperus virginiana*), 58; one-seed juniper (*Juniperus monosperma*), 11; 'Skyrocket' juniper (*Juniperus scopulorum*), 108

Katherine Mather Simms Award for English Composition (University of New Mexico), 41
katsura trees (*Cercidiphyllum japonicum*), 39
Keith, Susan, 85

Kentucky coffee tree *(Gymnocladus dioicus)*, 80
Kentucky wisteria (*W. macrostachya*), 55
Kimmerer, Robin Wall, 139
King, Sam, 21
King Brothers, Alamo Ranch, 21
Kinyanjui, Nancy, 136, 137
Kinyanjui, Susie, 136
kitchen gardens, 18, 29, 48, 62, 63
Kitts, J. R., 64–65

lacebark elms (*Ulmus parvifolia* 'Emer II'), 105–6, 108, 109
Lady Banks roses (*Rosa banksia* 'Alba' and 'Lutea'), *76*, 96, 101, 102, 148
La Glorieta (Albuquerque), 34
lagoon/pond, 74, *75*, 78–79, *93, 137,* 147. *See also* lotus pond
la merienda, 94
La Montañita Co-op, 76, 115
Lamy, Jean Baptiste (Archbishop), 17
Land and Water Summit (2021), 20–21
land grant schools, 18
landrace plants, 151–52
landscape architecture/design: birth and history of, 27–28; as collaborative discipline, 140; cultural shift in attitudes in, 135–36; importance of in evolution of Los Poblanos, 92; use of phrase, 22–23
The Landscape Gardening and Landscape Architecture of the Late Humphry Repton, Esq. (Louden), 28
Langstroth, L. L./Langstroth hives, *117*
La Quinta: as cultural center, 43–44, 82; farm-to-table banquets in, 94; galas at, 73; garden relationship between Los Poblanos hacienda and, 58–59; gardens of, 59–60; Grand Portal at.

See Grand Portal (La Quinta); as guest house and cultural center, 46; map of, *47*; new gardens surrounding, 105–6; Penny and Armin Rembe purchase of, 82; photo of, *106*; as rejoining Los Poblanos, 82–83
Las Acequias Farm (Nambe, New Mexico), 34–35
Lavandula × intermedia 'Grosso'/cultivars, 23, 84, 85
lavender: on display in Village Festival, 87; distillation of, *111*, 145–47; drying, 87; English lavender (*Lavandula angustifolia*), 85; 'Grosso' lavender (*Lavandula × intermedia*), 84–85, 105, 108, *123*; growing of, *86*, 113; harvest of, *86*; 'Hidcote' lavenders (*Lavandula angustifolia*), 85, 122; *Lavandula angustifolia*, 28; as pest-resistant crop that could be grown with limited water, 85; Portuguese or spike lavender (*Lavandula latifolia*), 85; 'Provence' lavandin, 84–85; 'Sharon Roberts' lavenders (*Lavandula angustifolia*), 85, 122
Lavender Day celebration (2004), 85
Lavender hand sanitizer, 141
Lavender in the Valley Festival, 85, 86, 95–96, *111*
lavender product line, 115, 116, 136, 141, *142*
lavender salve, 115
lawns: ceremonial/wedding garden lawn, 105, 108; cult of, 18; hacienda lawn, *107*; limiting of, 60; use of in colonial times, 4
lemon balm (*Melissa officinalis*), 100
Lenten rose (*Helleborus orientalis*), 81
lettuce, looseleaf lettuce (*Lactuca sativa*), *121*

Manning, Warren H., 29

manzanita, hybrid manzanitas (*Arcto-staphylos × coloradensis*), 123

Manzano Day School (Albuquerque), 34, 65, 69

maple: Japanese maple (*Acer palmatum*), 55; silver maple (*Acer saccharinum*), 61

marigolds (*Tagetes*, 49): signet marigolds (*Tagetes tenuifolia*), 78

mariposa lily (*Calochortus*), 49

market-driven preservation paradigm, of Los Poblanos, 109–10, 116, 140

Martin, Paul S., 7

Martin, Robin McKinney and Meade, 34

Martin, Serrano, Antonio and Sebastian, 37–38

Martinez, Cleofia, 86

'Mary Wallace' (climbing rose), 49

matanza, 144, *145*

Mather, Increase, 41

'Maverick' honey mesquite (*Prosopis glandulosa*), 125

Maximilian sunflower (*Helianthus maximiliani*), 58

McCormick, Cyrus, III, 34

McCormick, John Medill, 65, 66–67

McCormick, Medill, 42

McCormick, Ruth Hanna (later Ruth Simms), 42

McElroy, John T., 36

McGlade, Dennis, 92, 94, 95, 106, 108–9, 118, 136

McHarg, Ian, 140

McKinney, Louise and Robert, 34

McSween, Susan, 36

Medici family, gardens of, 28

medicines: from cottonwoods, 8, *9*; examples of plants used for, 11, 28; from mullein, 122; from *Nicotiana*, *10*; salt

cedar as chelator of heavy metals, 58; tending plants for, 3, 7, 8, 23; from yerba mansa, *11*, 101, 127–28

Meeks, Stephanie, 110

Meem, John Gaw, 1, 2, 34, 43–44, 47, 48–49, 60, 63, 64, 74, 79, 80, 84, 91, 92, 100, 118, 147

Meem Suites, *93*, 94

Meidiland groundcover roses, 105

Mescalero Apaches, 14

Mesopotamia, ornamental gardens in, 27

mesquites (*Prosopsis* spp.), 11

Mexican threadgrass (*Nasella tenuissima*), *120*, 130, *131*

Michigan State University, degree in landscape architecture, 27

Middle Rio Grande Conservancy District (MRGCD), 16, 19, 20–21, 34, 107–8

milking barns, 62, 101, 118

milkweeds (*Asclepias* spp.), 11

Miller, Harry Garrison, *67*

Miller, Kristie, 42

Mimbres River, 36

mint: 'Ava's' hummingbird mint (*Agastache cana*), 132; bush mint (*Zizophora clinopodioides*), 100; licorice mint (*Agastache rupestris*), 100; spearmint (*Mentha spicata*), 100

mission (of Rembe family), 91

missionaries, fruit trees introduced by, 13

Mitchell, Albert, 65

Mogollon settlements, evidence of, 36

monasteries, gardens and botanical expertise in, 28

Monticello, gardens of, 29

Moore, James, 91

Moorish fountain, 49, *76*

Morgan, Julia, 32

Moule & Polyzoides, Architects and Urbanists, 92, *93*, 118

mountain ash (*Sorbus americana*), 50

Mudejar, 51, 152

mulberry (*Morus* spp., 27): *Morus alba*, 28, 36; weeping mulberry tree (*Morus alba* 'Pendula'), 100–101, 123

mullein (*Verbascum thapsus*), *120*, 121

mums (*Chrysanthemum* cultivars), 62

mural, 84

musk rose (*Rosa moschata*), 56

mycorrhizae, 129, 137, 152

Na-Fiat Sandia Puebloans, 1

Nanking cherries (*Prunus tomentosa* var. *Leucocarpa*), 39

NAN Ranch (Faywood, New Mexico), 36

narrow-leafed boxwood (*Buxus* spp.), 80

nasturtium (*Tropaeolum* cultivars), 145

National Trust for Historic Preservation, Trustees Emeritus Aware for Excellence in the Stewardship of Historic Sites, 109–10

native grasses, 134, *134*, 135

native honey mesquite (*Prosopis glandulosa*), 13

Native peoples. *See* Indigenous people

native plants: adaptive evolution of, 36; advocacy for use of, 18, 22, 24; blending of with exotics, 131; blending of with regional natives and adapted exotics, 62; cultivation of useful one, 3; displacement of, 17; edible ones, 121; estates as stripped of, 4; use of, 23, 45, 110, 118

native valley cottonwoods (*Populus deltoides* spp. *wislizeni*), 8, *9*, 17, 49, 58, 80, 100, 130